The Respect for Fundamental Human Rights in the Fight against Human Trafficking and Migrant Smuggling across the Central Mediterranean Sea

Transnational Crime

Volumes published in this Brill Research Perspective are listed at *brill.com/rptc*

The Respect for Fundamental Human Rights in the Fight against Human Trafficking and Migrant Smuggling across the Central Mediterranean Sea

By

Laura Salvadego

TUTA SUB AEGIDE PALLAS · 1683 ·

BRILL

LEIDEN | BOSTON

This paperback book edition is simultaneously published as issue 1.4 of *Transnational Crime*, DOI:10.1163/24680931-12340009.

Library of Congress Control Number: 2019947307

Typeface for the Latin, Greek, and Cyrillic scripts: "Brill". See and download: brill.com/brill-typeface.

ISBN 978-90-04-40834-0 (paperback)
ISBN 978-90-04-40835-7 (e-book)

This book is printed on acid-free paper and produced in a sustainable manner.

Contents

The Respect for Fundamental Human Rights in the Fight against Human Trafficking and Migrant Smuggling across the Central Mediterranean Sea

Laura Salvadego
Researcher of International Law, University of Macerata
laura.salvadego@unimc.it

Abstract

This study analyzes counter-smuggling and counter-trafficking operations carried out in the Mediterranean, mainly focusing on the EU operations *Sophia* and *Themis*. The purpose is to assess a number of issues linked with naval operations from a human rights perspective. These issues include the applicable law, the exercise of criminal jurisdiction over smugglers and traffickers, national strategies of coastal States as regards migration control policy and, finally, international responsibility for human rights violations perpetrated in connection with these operations. Although the study is primarily aimed at both Ph.D students and legal scholars specialized in the field, it also seeks to provide insights that may be of guidance to NGOs, legal practitioners and legislators within the EU and its Member States.

Keywords

EUNAVFOR MED Operation *Sophia* – Frontex Operation *Themis* – criminal jurisdiction – humanitarian activities at sea – international responsibility – monitoring mechanisms

•••

To Filippo

 | DOI:10.1163/9789004408357_002

Introduction

The large-scale transnational mobility of migrants[1] affects different geographical areas.[2] One of the routes most often in the spotlight of the international community is the Central Mediterranean.[3] The flows of migrants seeking to penetrate into the Schengen area by sea from Northern Africa, Libya in particular, increased rapidly following the 'Arab Spring' of 2011 and have more recently reached a peak due to the armed conflicts raging in Libya, Syria and Iraq. People smugglers take advantage of the situation to exploit migrants in order to gain substantial economic benefits.

The deposition and subsequent execution of Gadaffi in 2011 inaugurated a new phase of political instability in the area, which has since led to an intensification of the clashes among different local tribes fighting one another for control over the territory. It was not until the end of 2015 that a partial stabilization of the area was achieved with the establishment of a Government of National Accord headed by Serraj, which has received support from the United Nations (UN),[4] but still controls only part of the Libyan territory. Since 2011, in fact, Libya has not been able to exert any effective control over its external borders, carry out the necessary inspections of vessels flying the State flag or registered in the country[5] or guarantee the correct functioning of the Coast

1 In this paper, the term is used in reference to people who leave their country of origin, without distinction based on the status ascribable to them under international law, and includes asylum seekers, refugees and economic migrants. For a full examination of definition issues see, among others, Julian Lehmann, "Rights at the Frontier: Border Control and Human Rights Protection of Irregular International Migrants," *Goettingen Journal of International Law* 3 (2011): 373 and UNHCR, "Handbook on Procedures and Criteria for Determining Refugee Status under the 1951 Convention and the 1967 Protocol relating to the Status of Refugees," UN Doc HCR/IP/4/Eng/REV.1, January 1992, para. 62.

2 See the Report of the Secretary-General of the UN, "In Safety and Dignity: Addressing Large Movements of Refugees and Migrants," April 21, 2016, UN Doc. A/70/59, para. 1.

3 For a detailed illustration of the land, air and sea routes used to smuggle migrants into the European Union (EU), see European Commission, "A Study on Smuggling of Migrants. Characteristics, Responses and Cooperation with Third Countries: Final Report," September 2015, 37.

4 See Security Council Resolution No. 2259 (2015), December 23, 2015, UN Doc. S/RES/2259, para. 3.

5 Cf. Article 94 of the UN Convention on the Law of the Sea (UNCLOS), concluded in Montego Bay on December 10, 1982, in force as of November 16, 1994, *UNTS* vol. 1833, 3. The EU has been a party to the UNCLOS since April 1, 1998, with reference to the matters in respect of which competence was transferred (Articles 4 and 5 of Annex IX of the UNCLOS). Libya signed the UNCLOS on December 3, 1984, but did not subsequently ratify it. However, the obligation in question codifies a general norm that all States of the international community must abide by. Regarding the customary nature of a large

Guard and rescue operations in its search and rescue region (SRR).[6] This situation has created conditions for the proliferation of criminal networks dedicated to migrant smuggling, often endowed with branches in Europe and facilitated by collusive practices that are widespread among Libyan officials.[7] Consequently, migrant smugglers are able to operate, mostly undisturbed, both within the territory of the State and in its territorial waters, often also on the high seas.

Generally speaking, in fact, third States cannot make up for the deficiencies of the Libyan Coast Guard. For one thing, only the coastal State can exert police powers in its territorial waters and, *a fortiori*, on its territory. Moreover, transnational human trafficking[8] and migrant smuggling[9]—defined, respectively, in the Trafficking Protocol and Smuggling Protocol, both annexed to the 2000 UN Convention on Transnational Organized Crime (UNTOC)[10]—do not *per se* constitute crimes *iuris gentium*.[11] And this circumstance is not without consequences as regards the possibility of taking action against ships that engage in these unlawful activities on the high seas.

---

part of the norms codified in the Convention, see ICJ, *Continental Shelf* (*Libyan Arab Jamahiriya v Malta*), judgment of June 3, 1985, *ICJ Reports*, 1985, 13, para. 26.

6 Cf. Article 98 UNCLOS; Libya is not party to the UNCLOS, but it did accede to the SAR Convention in 2005: see IMO, SAR/Circ. 77, May 17, 2005, Ref. A1/W/2.03. After a period of uncertainty, on August 10, 2018 the Libyan Navy announced the establishment of a Libyan SRR in accordance with the 1979 SAR Convention. The Libyan SRR currently coincides with the Tripoli Flight Information Region (FIR), already notified to the International Civil Aviation Organization. See Global Integrated Shipping Information System, https://gisis.imo.org/Public/Default.aspx (last accessed May 13, 2019).

7 Again European Commission, "A Study on Smuggling," 39.

8 Cf. Article 3(a) Trafficking Protocol.

9 Cf. Article 3(a) Smuggling Protocol.

10 UN Convention against Transnational Organized Crime (UNTOC), adopted by the UN General Assembly in New York on November 15, 2000 with Resolution No. 55/25 (2000), in force since September 29, 2003, *UNTS* vol. 2225, 209; Protocol against Smuggling of Migrants by Land, Sea and Air annexed to the Convention (Smuggling Protocol), adopted in New York on November 15, 2000, *UNTS* vol. 2241, 507, in force since January 28, 2004. There are 145 Parties to the Protocol, including the EU, since September 6, 2006. Libya signed the Protocol on November 13, 2001 and ratified it on September 24, 2004. Protocol to Prevent, Suppress and Punish Trafficking in Persons, Especially Women and Children, supplementing the Convention (Trafficking Protocol), adopted in New York on November 15, 2000, *UNTS* vol. 2237, 319, in force since December 25, 2003.

11 In this regard, see Anne Gallagher and Fiona David, *The International Law of Migrant Smuggling* (Cambridge: CUP, 2014), 246 and 423–426. With respect to human trafficking see, however, "Sixteenth Report of the Prosecutor of the International Criminal Court to the United Nations Security Council Pursuant to UNSCR 1970 (2011)," paras. 26, 32–35, https://www.icc-cpi.int/itemsDocuments/181102-rep-otp-UNSC-libya_ENG.pdf (last accessed June 21, 2019).

Firstly, a State other than the flag State cannot, as a rule, seize any vessel intercepted on the high seas that is being used for this unlawful activity, arrest its crew or prosecute those responsible, as is permitted, by contrast, under the UN Convention on the Law of the Sea (UNCLOS) in relation to activities of piracy on the high seas.[12] Third States only have the right to visit, provided that the conditions established by Article 110 UNCLOS are met. In actual fact, a State other than the flag State can exercise the right to visit a ship on the high seas only if the flag State gives its consent—either under an international agreement or by virtue of a unilateral act (Article 110(1))—or if the ship is without nationality (Article 110(1)(d)). Moreover, Article 8 Smuggling Protocol largely reiterates the general discipline codified in the UNCLOS.

The same still holds true as regards the trafficking in persons, which does not seem to fall within the scope of Article 110(1)(b) UNCLOS; the latter allows the exercise of the right of visit in the case of foreign ships suspected of being engaged in the 'slave trade', but makes no mention of trafficking. The clear distinction between 'slavery' and 'trafficking in human beings' was also highlighted by the European Court of Human Rights (ECtHR) in the *Rantsev* case.[13]

Consequently, migrant smuggling and human trafficking by sea cannot fall within the jurisdiction of any State other than the coastal State, flag State or the State in which the ship was registered.[14] Furthermore, under general international law, only the coastal State is allowed to exercise policing functions in territorial waters; as a consequence, no ship of a third State could follow a vessel engaging in this unlawful activity into the territorial waters of a different

12 See Article 105 UNCLOS. More will be said below, Part II, para. 7.2 and Part III.

13 ECtHR, *Rantsev v Cyprus and Russia*, Appl. No. 25965/04, judgment of January 7, 2010, para. 272. *Contra* see, among others, Giorgia Bevilacqua, *Criminalità e sicurezza in alto mare* (Naples: Scientifica, 2017), 146.

14 The obligation of a coastal State to guarantee the safety and security of its territorial waters was affirmed by the ICJ in the case of the Strait of Corfù: *The Corfu Channel Case (United Kingdom v Albania)*, judgment of April 9, 1949, *ICJ Reports*, 1949, 22. Jurisdiction entails the power of States to create and impose rules. This power may assume different forms. Firstly, *prescriptive jurisdiction* is the power of a State to create legal norms regulating conduct; secondly, *enforcement jurisdiction* is the power of a State to apply its rules through coercive action directed against persons and objects; finally, *adjudicative jurisdiction* is the power of a State to decide, through its judges, on the interpretation and application of legal rules. On the issue see Irini Papanicolopulu, *International Law and the Protection of People at Sea* (Oxford: OUP, 2018), 115.

State.[15] The persisting political instability in Libya, mentioned earlier, and of the entire North African region, has also long precluded—until recent times[16]—the possibility of entering into *ad hoc* agreements for joint patrols of the area[17] or of implementing those concluded previously.[18]

In light of the above-described situation, the international community soon realised that, given the vast entity of the phenomenon and the consequent endangerment of the life of migrants, a coordinated strategy of action was called for. The European Union (EU), in particular, decided to launch a military operation—EUNAVFOR MED Operation *Sophia* (Operation *Sophia*)—whose objective was to "disrupt the business model of human smuggling and trafficking networks in the Southern Central Mediterranean".[19] Under the original plan, the operation was supposed to be implemented in three successive stages, which would involve the high seas and Libya's territorial waters and territory, including its internal waters.[20] Furthermore, the EU also activated joint missions in the area, coordinated by the new Frontex Agency (Operations *Triton* and *Themis*),[21] and the NATO is conducting a maritime security operation.

---

15 Cf. Article 111(3) UNCLOS, which codifies a general rule in this regard: see Robin Greiβ and Anna Petrig, *Piracy and Armed Robbery at Sea. The Legal Framework for Counter-Piracy Operations in Somalia and the Gulf of Aden* (Oxford: OUP, 2011), 67.

16 On this issue, see below, Part IV, para. 1.

17 An analogous solution has been implemented by Malaysia, Indonesia and Singapore to combat the phenomenon of piracy in the Malacca Strait: cf. Catherine Zara Raymond, "Piracy and Armed Robbery in the Malacca Strait. A Problem Solved?," *Naval War College Review* 62 (2009): 36.

18 The reference is to bilateral agreements concluded between Italy and Libya for the joint management of migratory flows from Libya: cf. Treaty of Friendship, Partnership and Cooperation between the Italian Republic and the Great Socialist People's Libyan Arab Jamahiriya, Benghazi, August 30, 2008. As of 2011 they were suspended due to Security Council Resolution No. 1973 (2011), which launched Operation *Unified Protector*. On this subject see Mariagiulia Giuffrè, "State Responsibility beyond Borders: What Legal Basis for Italy's Push-Backs to Libya?," *International Journal of Refugee Law* 24 (2012): 695.

19 Decision No. 2015/778/CFSP of the Council, May 18, 2015, concerning a military operation of the European Union in the southern Central Mediterranean (EUNAVFOR MED), *OJEU* L 122, 31, recital 5 and Article 1(1).

20 See again Decision No. 2015/778/CFSP, Article 2(2)(a), (b) and (c).

21 Frontex (*European Border and Coast Guard Agency*) is an EU Agency established in 2004 with Council Regulation No. 2007/2004, October 26, 2004 (*OJEU* L 349, 1), with the aim of improving cooperation among national border agencies. The Agency coordinates naval interdiction activities, established by the EU for the purpose of external border control. Its founding regulation was amended with Regulation No. 2016/1624, September 14, 2016

Irregular migration, as known, may generate a number of very different human rights concerns in all phases of the migration process.[22] The same holds true with respect to counter-smuggling and counter-trafficking operations at sea. As the migration crisis has once more confirmed, in fact, external border control is inherently human rights sensitive. This is so regardless of whether States control their borders alone, jointly, or with the assistance of international or supranational organizations.[23]

As over four years have elapsed since the counter-smuggling and counter-trafficking operations at sea began, it is now possible to assess the results of the fight against migrant smuggling and people trafficking across the Mediterranean. This book aims first of all to clarify the legal basis of the operations undertaken in the Central Mediterranean (Part I, para. 2); it subsequently examines the command and control structure of Operation *Sophia* and of Frontex joint operations (Part I, paras. 3–4) and the rules for attributing unlawful conduct in the context of these missions (Part I, para. 5). The applicable law is then considered in Part II, with a particular focus on the protection of the fundamental human rights of both migrants and the persons involved in the unlawful activities at sea (paras. 6–12). Part III focuses on the exercise of criminal jurisdiction over the smugglers and traffickers caught during law enforcement operations in the Mediterranean. Part IV briefly analyzes the strategies adopted by Italy in this scenario and their implications in a human rights perspective. The book then concludes by examining the issue of international responsibility for the violation of fundamental human rights during naval operations at sea (Part V). It is not always straightforward to establish whether responsibility for the unlawful conducts engaged in during operations in the area should be attributed to the individual State taking part in the multinational mission or to the international organization that set up or authorized the mission. As regards to all of these aspects, our analysis mainly focuses on the EU operations *Sophia* and *Themis*.

(*OJEU* L 251, 1). See, generally, Roberta Mungianu, "Frontex: Towards a Common Policy on External Border Control," *European Journal of Migration and Law* 15 (2013): 359. Below, Part I, para. 3.

22 See Jorge Bustamante, "Report of the Special Rapporteur on the Human Rights of Migrants," UN Doc A/HRC/7/12, February 25, 2008, para. 15.

23 Melanie Fink, "Salami Slicing Human Rights Accountability: How the European Border and Coast Guard Agency may inherit Frontex' genetic defect," *EJIL: Talk!*, March 10, 2016.

Part I. The Naval Operations in the Central Mediterranean: Main Features

1 *The Legal Basis of Naval Operations in the Central Mediterranean*

The Security Council has been addressing the phenomenon of migrant trafficking and smuggling across the Mediterranean since May 2015, when the High Representative of the Union for Foreign Affairs and Security Policy informed the Council of the EU's intention to undertake a naval operation to confront the migrant 'crisis' in the Mediterranean and highlighted the need to obtain the support of the Security Council.[24] The Council feared that the situation in the Mediterranean might exacerbate the unstable situation in Libya, which had already previously been qualified as a threat to international peace and security.[25] However, it was only after an explicit request from the Libyan Government of National Accord that the Security Council authorized the Member States to conduct—also through international organizations—the operations designed to combat criminal networks in international waters off the Libyan coasts.[26]

The fleet presently engaged in the area is a composite one and includes a group of States acting individually[27] and three multinational missions: Operation *Sophia*,[28] Frontex Operation *Themis*,[29] which, starting from February 2018, replaced Operation *Triton*, and NATO's Operation *Sea Guardian*,

---

24 Cf. Giovanni Faleg and Steven Blockmans, "EU Naval Force EUNAVFOR MED Sets Sail in Troubled Waters," June 26, 2015, www.ceps.eu (last accessed April 18, 2019), 3; on the need for prior authorization by the UN Security Council in the case of missions entailing the use of armed force see, generally, Micaela Frulli, *Le operazioni di peacekeeping delle Nazioni Unite: continuità di un modello normativo* (Naples: Scientifica, 2012), 22.

25 See, among others, Security Council Resolution No. 2238 (2015), September 10, 2015.

26 See Security Council Resolution No. 2240 (2015), October 9, 2015, paras. 7–8 and 10.

27 Thus, e.g., the Italian mission *Mare Sicuro* was launched in the area in 2015: cf. the hearing of Admiral Credendino before the Italian Parliament, stenographic record No. 18 of February 4, 2016, www.camera.it, 7 (last accessed April 18, 2019). On August 2, 2017 the Chamber of Deputies and Senate authorized a partial amendment to the mandate of operation *Mare Sicuro*, which currently performs limited functions of support to the Libyan Coast Guard in the territorial waters of that State (operation NAURAS): see stenographic record No. 847, August 2, 2017, www.camera.it, 4 (last accessed April 18, 2019). See below, Part IV, para. 1.

28 Again see Decision No. 2015/778/CFSP. Its mandate was extended until September 2019; however, it was decided to recall the naval fleet from the Mediterranean: cf. https://www.operationsophia.eu/ (last accessed April 24, 2019).

29 Cf. www.frontex.europa.eu (last accessed April 24, 2019).

which, starting from November 2016, replaced Operation *Active Endeavour*.[30] Despite the efforts made to coordinate the different missions, each operation is characterised by a distinct composition and mandate and has an autonomous chain of command.[31]

While Operations *Sea Guardian* and *Themis* follow the general rules codified under the UNCLOS, special rules regulate Operation *Sophia*, especially as regards the possibility of intercepting ships flying the flag of third States. Operation *Sophia* has a dual legal basis: on the one hand, the authorization of the Security Council, adopted under Chapter VII of the UN Charter for an initial period of one year[32] and periodically renewed;[33] and, on the other hand, the consent of the Libyan Government of National Accord.[34] More precisely, Resolution No. 2240 (2015) expressly establishes that operations involving vessels on the high seas may be carried out only by States (and international organizations) that have obtained the consent of the flag State[35] or that have in any case made "good faith efforts to obtain the consent of the vessel's flag State"[36]—in the event that the request for consent to intervene remains unanswered—"in a rapid and timely manner".[37] Consequently, the resolution extends to some degree the possibility of intervention in the course of operations at sea allowed under general international law, enabling States to exercise the right to inspect vessels believed to be engaging in the above-mentioned illegal activities in the area and seize the vessels actually being used for migrant smuggling.

The consent of the Libyan Government of National Accord should also be sought, *a fortiori*, in the event of an authorization to engage in analogous operations in territorial and inland waters and within the territory of the State. Though such consent is not strictly necessary for the operations decided on the basis of Chapter VII of the Charter, it is nonetheless preferable in order not to weaken the authority of the fragile Libyan authorities.[38] Moreover, the

30 See the NATO official website: www.nato.int/cps/en/natohq/topics_7932.htm (last accessed April 18, 2019); see again stenographic record No. 18, 11.

31 Ibid., 7.

32 Cf. Security Council Resolution No. 2240 (2015), paras. 7–8.

33 Ibid., para. 19.

34 Ibid., para. 2.

35 Ibid., paras. 6–7.

36 Ibid., para. 7.

37 Cf. Security Council Resolution No. 2240 (2015), para. 9; on this subject see Marco Gestri, "EUNAVFOR MED: Fighting Migrant Smuggling under UN Security Council Resolution 2240 (2015)," *Italian Yearbook of International Law* 25 (2016): 38–40.

38 For analogous considerations concerning the consent of the Somalian government in the fight against piracy in Somalia see Tullio Treves, "Piracy, Law of the Sea, and Use of Force:

adoption of a resolution allowing operations to be conducted in the area without the local government's approval would be frowned upon by other African States.[39]

As noted earlier, however, a broad area of Libyan territory has not yet been brought under the control of Libya's Unity Government.[40] Consequently, in the absence of an *ad hoc* authorization of the UN Security Council, the validity of any consent expressed by the government might be disputed, thus undermining the legitimacy of the operations.[41] An analogous solution had been adopted under the Security Council's authorization of the anti-piracy initiatives carried out within the framework of the EU EUNAVFOR Operation *Atalanta* in the territorial waters of Somalia and later also in the territory and inland waters of that State:[42] in 2008, in fact, the Somali transition Government did not exert full control over the territory of the State.[43]

2 *The Command and Control Structure of* EUNAVFOR MED *Operation* Sophia

Like the other military operations of the EU,[44] Operation *Sophia* was undertaken on the basis of Articles 42 and 43 of the Treaty on European Union (TEU).[45] Under Article 42(4) TEU, all decisions regarding the Common Security and Defence Policy (CSDP)—which forms an integral part of the Common Foreign and Security Policy (CFSP) of the EU[46]—including military operations,

---

Developments off the Coast of Somalia," *European Journal of International Law* 20 (2009): 406.

39 Again see stenographic record No. 18, 6 and 10–11.

40 See above, Introduction.

41 Similar conclusions regarding the resolution on piracy off the Somalian coast are reached by Alessandra Annoni, "International Action against Piracy and Armed Robbery at Sea Off the Coast of Somalia," *Italian Yearbook of International Law* 23 (2013): 180 and Antonello Tancredi, "Di pirati e Stati 'falliti': il Consiglio di sicurezza autorizza il ricorso alla forza nelle acque territoriali della Somalia," *Rivista di diritto internazionale* 91 (2008): 944.

42 Decision No. 2008/851/CFSP, November 10, 2008, concerning the military operation of the European Union aimed at helping to deter, prevent and repress acts of piracy and armed robbery off the coast of Somalia, *OJEU* L 301, 33.

43 Cf. again Annoni, "International," 180.

44 For the essential elements of the military and civilian operations conducted by the EU, see generally Gaspare Fiengo, "Brevi note sulle 'missioni' dell'Unione europea per la gestione di crisi internazionali," *Il diritto dell'Unione Europea* 4 (2016): 551 and Panos Koutrakos, *The EU Common Security and Defence Policy* (Oxford: OUP, 2013).

45 Cf. Decision No. 2015/778/CFSP, Preamble.

46 Regarding the amendments introduced by the Treaty of Lisbon to the institutional order of the EU, see generally Roberto Baratta, "Le principali novità del Trattato di Lisbona," *Il diritto dell'Unione Europea* 13 (2008): 21.

must be adopted unanimously by the Council on a proposal from the High Representative of the Union for Foreign Affairs and Security Policy or an initiative from a Member State. Article 43(2) TEU specifies that military operations are decided by the Council, which establishes their objectives and scope and the general conditions for their implementation. The High Representative of the Union for Foreign Affairs and Security Policy, who acts under the authority of the Council and in close contact with the Political and Security Committee, will further ensure coordination of the civilian and military aspects of the mission.

The Council and the High Representative of the EU exercise oversight over Operation *Sophia* through the political control and strategic direction of the Political and Security Committee,[47] which is endowed with rather broad decision-making power. In practice, this means that all Member States can exercise a certain degree of control over the operations from a political-strategic standpoint: the voting mechanism within the Political and Security Committee operates according to the rule of unanimity.[48] The operation is thus characterised by a strong intergovernmental nature and does not respond to the European Parliament.[49] In any event, the Parliament performs a wholly marginal role within the framework of the CFSP: it is vested solely with an advisory function in the case of agreements to be concluded between the EU and third States or with international organizations linked to the CFSP.[50] The possibility of agreements of this sort is moreover envisaged by the establishing decision inaugurating Operation *Sophia*.[51] However, any contribution of third States will prejudice neither the EU's decision-making autonomy nor the unitary institutional framework.[52] Operation *Sophia* is further authorized to provide information on ongoing operations both to the UN and third States.[53]

47 Cf. Decision No. 2015/778/CFSP, para. 10 and Article 6(1).

48 Frederik Naert, "The Application of International Humanitarian Law and Human Rights in CSDP Operations," in *International Law as the Law of European Union*, eds. Enzo Cannizzaro, Paolo Palchetti and Ramses Wessel (Leiden: Nijhoff, 2012), 192.

49 For some critical remarks, see Isabella Mercone, "Some Notes on the Relations between UNSC Resolution 2240 (2015) Fighting Smugglers in Mediterranean and the EUNAVFOR MED 'Sophia' Operation," *European Area of Freedom Security and Justice*, FREE Group, October 19, 2015.

50 Cf. Article 218 TFEU and CJEU, GC, case C-658/11, *European Parliament v Council*, judgment of June 24, 2014.

51 Cf. Decision No. 2015/778/CFSP, Article 9(1) and 9(2).

52 Ibid., Article 9(1).

53 Ibid., Article 12.

With regard to the structure of the mission, the EU has developed an 'autonomous' concept of command and control.[54] The EU is not endowed in any case with military command structures of a permanent character. The Military Committee of the EU does not belong to the chain of command of the military operations established within the framework of the CSDP; its role is limited to supervision and monitoring of the correct implementation of such missions.[55] For its own part, the Political and Security Committee only exercises political control and oversees strategic direction of crisis management operations; consequently, the military control of each mission is determined separately on the basis of *ad hoc* agreements.[56]

The operations established by the Council are characterised by a unitary command structure: in fact, the Council has overall responsibility for their conduct.[57] The EU thus plays a central strategic role, which imposes, among other things, a transfer of authority over the military contingents that States place at the disposal of the mission commander on a voluntary basis.[58] It is precisely this transfer of authority which allows the mission commander to exercise operational control over the forces provided by the individual States taking part: the EU lays down the general principles; detailed rules are then established by *ad hoc* agreements with individual States providing forces.[59]

However, the EU's freedom in managing individual national contingents is to some extent limited by the possible placement of specific national caveats.[60] For the most part, these caveats are formulated at the time of the transfer of authority, but nothing prevents them from being introduced later in the course of the operation.[61] This means that the contributing States exercise a certain degree of *de facto* control over their respective contingents and have a concrete possibility of influencing the conduct of military operations to some extent.

---

54 Cf. Council of the EU, "European Union Concept for Military Command and Control," Doc. 5008/15, January 5, 2015.

55 Cf. Decision No. 2001/79 of the Council, January 22, 2001, *OJEU* L 27, 4.

56 Cf. Frederik Naert, *International Law Aspects of the EU's Security and Defence Policy, with a Particular Focus on the Law of Armed Conflict* (Antwerp: Intersentia, 2010), 61–62.

57 See again Council of the EU, "European Union Concept," 9, para. 11.

58 Ibid., 11, para. 11(f).

59 Cf. Bundesverfassungericht, *Lissabon Urteil*, case no. BvE 2/08, judgment of June 30, 2009, para. 387, https://www.bundesverfassungsgericht.de (last accessed April 18, 2019), regarding which see Lucia Serena Rossi, "La sentenza del Bundesverfassungericht sul Trattato di Lisbona e le implicazioni sul processo di integrazione europea," in *Studi degli allievi di Paolo Mengozzi*, eds. Lucia Serena Rossi and Elisa Baroncini (Naples: Scientifica, 2010), 91.

60 Ibid., 12, para. 11(h).

61 Ibid., paras. 22 and 28.

From an operational viewpoint, the highest level of strategic-military command over the Operation *Sophia*, as well as command over the operational and tactical aspects, has been entrusted to two Italian commanders—respectively the Operation Commander and the Force Commander—both exponents of the 'framework nation' that has taken responsibility for directing and planning the operation.[62] This means that Italy has organized the headquarters of the operation and placed its own command and control structures at the latter's disposal. This circumstance does not, however, assign Italy a 'pre-eminent' role *vis-à-vis* other contributing States in the conduct of the operations in the Central Mediterranean and has no particular consequences for the applicable regime of responsibility.[63] Moreover, the two commanders are fully incorporated into the EU chain of command. The Operation Commander interacts with the political-strategic bodies, submits periodic reports to the Council on the ongoing operations[64] and has operational control over the troops assigned by the contributing States by virtue of the previously discussed transfer of authority. The Force Commander, by contrast, represents the level closest to the contingents deployed in the area of the operations and exercises command and control of all field military forces.[65] This choice seems to have been motivated by the proximity to the theatre of the naval operations, as well as the need to ensure the best coordination between the EU operation and the national authorities responsible for the SAR activities in that maritime area.[66]

3 *The Command and Control Structure of Frontex Operations*

Operation *Sophia*, however, is not the only EU operation in the area. In fact, alongside this military operation, the EU has acted through its Agency Frontex. Due to the refugee crisis, the Proposal made by the Commission in December 2015 to create a European Border and Coast Guard (EBCG)[67] soon became legislation with Regulation No. 2016/1624 adopted in record time with a large consensus. While the EBCG replaces the European Agency for the Management of Operational Cooperation at the External Borders of the

62 See again Decision No. 2015/778/CFSP, Articles 3 and 4.
63 See below, Part I, para. 4 and Part V, para. 1.
64 See again Council of the EU, "European Union Concept," 25, para. 30.
65 Regarding the functioning of the chain of command and control in military operations undertaken within the framework of the CSDP, see Council of the EU, "EU Military C2 Concept," July 3, 2003, Doc. 11096/03 EXT 1, July 26, 2006, 6–7 and 15–16.
66 See below, Part II, para. 3.
67 European Commission, Proposal for a regulation of the European Parliament and of the Council on the European Border and Coast Guard and repealing Regulation No. 2007/2004, Regulation No. 863/2007 and Council Decision No. 2005/267/EC, Strasbourg, December 15, 2015, COM(2015) 671 final.

Member States of the EU, it has the same legal personality and the same 'short name'. Frontex, however, does not currently possess an international legal personality distinct and independent from that of the EU, which still represents the sole legal entity acting as the bearer of relevant rights and duties under international law.[68] A relevant confirmation of this argument may be seen in the Draft Agreement on the Accession of the EU to the European Convention for the Protection of Human Rights and Fundamental Freedoms (ECHR).[69] The Draft Agreement, indeed, expressly established that the ECHR could "impose on the European Union obligations with regard only to acts, measures or omissions of its institutions, bodies, offices, agencies, or of persons acting on their behalf."[70]

Wrongly considered as an ambitious solution, the EBCG has not proved capable of overcoming the structural limits highlighted by the Agency, especially as regards the controversial issue of international responsibility for human rights violations committed during joint operations of the Agency. Firstly, this new Agency remains intergovernmental and it does not guarantee independence towards Member States. Most of the decision-making competence, in fact, belongs to the Member States through the Management Board and to the Executive Director appointed by the Management Board and accountable to him.[71] Secondly, although the Commission purported to share border controls between the EU and its Member States, the latter remain responsible for their implementation, which is in contradiction with the principle of solidarity established by Article 80 TFEU,[72] with the consequence that

68 Cf. also, in this respect, Melanie Fink, "Frontex Working Arrangements: Legitimacy and Human Rights Concerns Regarding 'Technical Relationships'," *Merkourios* 28 (2012): 26; Pieter Jan Kuijper and Esa Paasivirta, "EU International Responsibility and Its Attribution: From the Inside Looking Out," in *The International Responsibility of the European Union. European and International Perspectives*, ed. Malcolm Evans and Panos Koutrakos (Oxford: Hart, 2013), 50. *Contra* see Gregor Schusterschitz, "European Agencies as Subjects of International Law," *International Organizations Law Review* 1 (2004): 169.

69 Convention for the Protection of Human Rights and Fundamental Freedoms (ECHR), Rome, November 4, 1950, in force since September 3, 1953, *UNTS* vol. 213, 221.

70 Article 1(3). Cf. Fifth Negotiation Meeting between the CDDH *ad hoc* Negotiation Group and the European Commission on the Accession of the EU to the European Convention on Human Rights, Final Report to the CDDH, 47+1(2013)008rev2, Strasbourg, June 10, 2013.

71 For an overview on the institutional framework and legal basis, see Mungianu, "Frontex," 374.

72 Regarding the principle of solidarity among States Members of the EU, see generally Marco Gestri, "La politica europea dell'immigrazione: solidarietà tra Stati membri e misure nazionali di regolarizzazione," in *Problemi e tendenze del diritto internazionale dell'economia. Liber amicorum in onore di Paolo Picone*, eds. Aldo Ligustro and Giorgio Sacerdoti (Naples: Scientifica, 2011), 895.

the funding of the European borders policy remains an unsolved problem.[73] In order to better protect the European free movement area, the Agency has now reinforced the powers of control over people entering at the external borders; however, the EBGC does not solve the structural problem of border controls in the EU, as it requires a centralised Agency for which there is no legal basis in the EU treaties.[74]

Thus, the new Frontex Regulation does not create a true 'European Border Guard' understood as an EU body made up of borders guards replacing national border guards.[75] In fact, national border guards remain almost untouched and this also has important consequences for the issue of solidarity inside the EU, which must be considered in conjunction with the allocation of responsibilities between the EU and its Member States.[76]

Despite the strengthening of the prerogatives of the Agency, border controls are in principle still implemented by each Member State individually. This is confirmed to some degree by Article 5 of the new Frontex regulation, according to which Member States shall retain 'primary responsibility' for the management of their sections of the external borders, in their own interests and in the common interest of all Member States.[77]

Setting up a joint operation at the external borders usually starts with a proposal made by a specific Member States which is scrutinised by Frontex.[78] However, the initiative with regard to the start of the operations may also come from Frontex itself.[79] The organizational aspects of the operations are covered by an 'operational plan', which is drawn up by Frontex's Executive Director and the host Member State, pursuant to Article 16(1) of Regulation No. 2016/1624. The other Member States participating in an operation only have a consultative role in the drawing up of the 'operational plan'.[80] The operational plan is binding on the Agency, the host Member State and the participating

73 On the EBCG and its limits, see further Philippe De Bruycker, "The European Border and Coast Guard: A New Model Built on an Old Logic," *European Papers* 1 (2016): 559.

74 Cf. Jorrit Rijpma, "The Proposal for a European Border and Coast Guard: Evolution or Revolution in External Border Management," *Libe Committee of the European Parliament*, 2016, 26.

75 The expression was firstly used by Sergio Carrera and Leonhard den Hertog, "A European Border and Coast Guard: What's in a Name?," *CEPS Paper in Liberty and Security in Europe*, March 8, 2016.

76 Cf. again De Bruycker, "The European," 565. On this issue more will be said below, Part I, para. 4 and Part V, para. 1.

77 Cf. Article 5(1) and 5(2) Regulation No. 2016/1624. Emphasis added.

78 Cf. Article 15(1) and Article 15(3) Regulation No. 2016/1624.

79 Article 15(4) Regulation No. 2016/1624.

80 Article 16(2) Regulation No. 2016/1624.

Member States and it covers all aspects considered necessary for carrying out the joint operation, including a description of the tasks and responsibilities also with regard to the respect for fundamental rights.[81]

During a joint operation, the EBGT—i.e. pools of border guards, including guest officers—are deployed.[82] The mechanism of deployment can be defined as 'on call', since the Frontex Regulation provides that the Member States are required to deploy the border guards at Frontex's request and not on a permanent basis.[83]

The host Member State is required to instruct the EBGT according to the 'operational plan'.[84] According to Article 21(2) of the Frontex Regulation, the Agency, through its coordinating officer, may communicate its views to the host Member State on the instructions given to the EBGT. In that case, the host Member State must take those views into consideration and follow them to the extent possible. The interface between Frontex and the host Member State and between Frontex and the members of the EBGT is the coordinating officer, an expert from the staff of Frontex, who acts on behalf of Frontex during the operations.[85] One of the coordinating officer's tasks is to monitor the correct implementation of the operational plan.[86]

Article 25 of the Frontex Regulation establishes the cases in which an operation may or must be terminated or suspended. The Executive Director must terminate an operation if the conditions for conducting it are no longer fulfilled, after informing the Member States concerned.[87] Furthermore, Member States participating in a specific operation, may request that the Executive Director terminate the operation.[88] Notably, the same provision states that, in cases in which the Executive Director determines the occurrence of violations of fundamental rights or of international protection obligations which are of a serious nature or are likely to persist, he or she is obliged to suspend or terminate the operation.[89]

---

81 Article 16(3) and 16(3)(d) Regulation No. 2016/1624.

82 Article 20(2) Regulation No. 2016/1624.

83 Cf. also Jorrit Rijpma, "Hybrid Agencification in the Area of Freedom, Security and Justice and Its Inherent Tensions: The Case of Frontex," in *The Agency Phenomenon in the European Union: Emergence, Institutionalization and Everyday Decision-Making*, ed. Madalina Busuioc *et al.* (Manchester: Manchester University Press, 2012), 84–102.

84 Article 21(1) Regulation No. 2016/1624.

85 Article 22 Regulation No. 2016/1624.

86 Article 22(3)(b) Regulation No. 2016/1624.

87 Article 25(1) Regulation No. 2016/1624.

88 Article 25(2) Regulation No. 2016/1624.

89 Article 25(4) Regulation No. 2016/1624.

Notwithstanding Member States' participation in all phases of the planning of the operations, the EU legal bases governing such operations give Frontex a leading role. The Agency is empowered by the Frontex Regulation to start an operation and to conduct a risk assessment on which the launching of the operation depends; the operational plan is drafted and amended by Frontex's Executive Director together with the Member States; Frontex contributes to the operation by communicating its views and through its coordinating officer; and Frontex's Executive Director can suspend or terminate the operation.

The description of the four aspects above shows that the role of Frontex is not limited to pure coordination. In fact, coordinating operations consist in assisting and supporting Member States only in cases in which technical and operational assistance is required by the latter. Yet, the role of Frontex is not only to support Member States' activities but also, to some extent, entails participation in the decision-making and direction of the operations.[90]

At the same time, however, even though border guards simultaneously fulfil a double function at national and EU level, they remain organically national as to their appointment; furthermore, salary, equipment, and also disciplinary measures correspond to a responsibility of each 'home' Member State.[91] In addition, in the context of Frontex operations, States do not make their assets available to the organization by transferring authority and control over them. Here, in fact, unlike the military operations of the EU, there is no real transfer of authority from the States to the organization. In this respect, it is possible to affirm that the Agency rather plays a role of coordinating States' activities and on this basis Frontex regularly argues that legal responsibility falls within the remit of Member States involved in joint operations.[92]

In this complex framework of relations between Member States and the Agency, it is of crucial importance to examine, whenever possible, the indications contained in the specific operational plan which establishes, in precise terms, the command and control structure of each individual mission.[93] Unfortunately, however, an examination of this instrument is not always possible due to the confidentiality often assigned to the operational plan of Frontex joint operations. This is precisely the case with the Frontex Operation *Themis*, established in February 2018 and replacing the previous

90 In this sense, see also Mungianu, "Frontex," 379.

91 Cf. Article 21(5) Regulation No. 2016/1624.

92 Cf. again Gallagher and David, *The International Law*, 342.

93 Cf. Article 16(3)(f) Regulation No. 2016/1624.

Frontex Joint Operation *Triton*, which had been launched in November 2014 at the request of Italy to assist the latter in patrolling the Central Mediterranean Sea. The operational plan was adopted jointly by the European Agency and the host State, but has not yet been made public. By analyzing Frontex official information on Operation *Themis*, however, it is possible to affirm that all assets deployed within the framework of this operation operate under the command of the host State (Italy) and the Agency only plays a role of coordinating and assisting of national efforts.[94] Thus, all the deployed guest officers work under the command and control of the authorities of the State hosting the operation. In practice this means that an officer from the host country is always present aboard every vessel, aircraft or patrol car deployed by Frontex.[95]

Unlike what it was established as a part of the Operation *Triton*, whose operational plan foresaw that any disembarkation would take place in Italy, the people rescued at sea as a part of Operation *Themis* are disembarked in the nearest safe harbor. Furthermore, the area of action of Operation *Themis* in the Central Mediterranean Sea has been limited to the 24 miles from the island of Lampedusa. Its mandate also includes a security component, including, for instance, steps aimed at detecting foreign fighters and other terrorist threats at the external borders.[96]

The assets currently involved in Operation *Themis*—like those previously involved in Operation *Triton*—now operate in strict compliance with the general rules of international law: Resolution No. 2240 (2015), in fact, did not lead to a modification of the operational plan of the missions coordinated by the European Agency. The ships allocated to Operation *Themis* can intercept and visit unflagged vessels suspected of being engaged in migrant smuggling only in international waters. Once their involvement in the unlawful activity is established, the Italian authorities are informed—as the authority of the country hosting the operation—so that they can adopt "further appropriate measures", either directly or with the assistance of the flag State of the ship that intercepted the vessel. The coercive measures include seizing and diverting the vessel and conducting the vessel with its cargo to the nearest safe harbor. However, in the case of vessels flying a foreign flag in international

94 All assets deployed within the framework of operation *Themis* operate under the command of the Italian Ministry of Interior: cf. https://frontex.europa.eu/along-eu-borders/main-operations/operation-themis-italy-/ (last accessed April 24, 2019).

95 See https://frontex.europa.eu/faq/frontex-operations/ (last accessed April 24, 2019).

96 Cf. https://frontex.europa.eu/along-eu-borders/main-operations/operation-themis-italy-/ (last accessed April 24, 2019).

waters, coercive measures may be adopted only with the authorization of the flag State, according to Regulation No. 2014/656, which is applicable to all the operations coordinated by Frontex.[97]

4 *The Attribution of Wrongful Conduct*

At this point of our analysis, it is possible to examine the legal framework concerning the attribution of wrongful conduct within the EU missions.

The practice related to peace-keeping operations set up by the UN has contributed to the modelling of a specific rule for attributing conduct in the case of State organs 'seconded' to an international organization. The reference here is to Article 7 of the 2011 Draft Articles on the Responsibility of International Organizations (DARIO).[98] In general, for the purpose of attributing wrongful conduct to the organization to which an organ of a State is seconded, the provision establishes the requirement that the organization have effective control over the specific conduct concerned.

Although, as mentioned, the general rule for attribution of responsibility is largely based on the practice related to UN operations,[99] the majority of legal commentators considers it also to be applicable within the framework of the military operations launched by the EU.[100] This is largely because of the numerous analogies that may be found in the operational model of the two types of missions.

In both cases, the Member States of the organization place their troops at the disposal of the mission, on a voluntary basis and for a certain interval of time, by concluding *ad hoc* agreements with the organization.[101] As a result, the troops seconded by contributing States have a 'dual' nature, in the sense

97 Article 7 Regulation No. 2014/656 on the surveillance of external sea borders.

98 Cf. Article 7 DARIO.

99 On this issue, cf. Giorgio Gaja, "Second Report on Responsibility of International Organizations," UN Doc. A/CN.4/541, April 2, 2004, 14.

100 Cf., among others, Paolo Palchetti, "International Responsibility for Conduct of UN Peacekeeping Forces: The Question of Attribution," in *Refining Human Rights Obligations in Conflict Situations*, ed. Paolo Palchetti (The Hague: Asser Press, 2014), 30; Ramses Wessel and Leonhard den Hertogh, "EU Foreign Security and Defence Policy: A Competence-Responsibility Gap?," in *The International Responsibility of the European Union: European and International Perspectives*, eds. Malcolm Evans and Panos Koutrakos (Oxford: Hart, 2013), 339. However, some scholars point out the rule of attribution established by Article 6 DARIO: see generally Aurel Sari and Ramses Wessel, "International Responsibility for EU Military Operations: Finding the EU's Place in the Global Accountability Regime," in *The EU's Role in Global Governance*, eds. Bart Van Vooren, Steven Blockmans and Jan Wouters (Oxford: OUP, 2013), 126.

101 Regarding the model of the peace-keeping operations of the UN, see generally Francesco Salerno, "International Responsibility for the Conduct of 'Blue Helmets': Exploring the

that, despite being part of the institutional system of the organization,[102] they simultaneously remain organs of the respective States that have sent them.[103]

In both cases, moreover, the link between the contributing States and their respective military contingents seconded to the organization cannot be said to have been completely severed. In concrete terms this means that, although the chain of command is fully and completely under the organization, the contributing States maintain exclusive competence in relation to some essential functions, including the training of their respective troops and the determination of the internal chain of command, as well as disciplinary and sanctioning powers.[104] Emblematic in this regard is Article 8 of the model Status of Forces Agreement (SOFA) provided for military operations established by the EU, which expressly attributes—exactly as in the case of UN peace-keeping operations—precise powers to the sending State in respect of disciplinary matters and sanctions to be applied to its troops.[105] As a rule, however, this applies only in the relationship between contributing States and the organization, without affecting the exclusive responsibility of the organization itself *vis-à-vis* third parties,[106] also in relation to conduct engaged in *ultra vires* by members of the mission.

Taken together, all of the elements considered lead us to conclude that the military operations of the EU are in line with the established model that is applied for UN peace-keeping operations. On the other hand, the military operations of the EU cannot be viewed as simple multilateral coalitions when the participating States autonomously manage the conduct of the operations. In such cases, the EU exercises a strategic and central role, including in the command and control structure. The transfer of authority by Member States

---

Organic Link," in *Responsibility of International Organizations. Essays in Memory of Sir Ian Brownlie*, ed. Maurizio Ragazzi (Leiden: Nijhoff, 2013), 415.

102 See generally Paulus, "Article 29," in *The Charter of the United Nations: A Commentary*, ed. Bruno Simma *et al.* (3rd edn. Oxford: OUP, 2012), 987.

103 Cf. Luigi Condorelli, "Le statut des forces de l'ONU et le droit humanitaire," *Rivista di diritto internazionale* 78 (1995), 881 and Gaja, "Second Report," para. 31.

104 See generally Robert Simmonds, *Legal Problems Arising from the United Nations Operation in the Congo* (The Hague: Nijhoff, 1986), 214.

105 Council of the EU, "Draft Model Agreement on the Status of the European Union-Led Forces between the European Union and a Host State," Doc. 11894/07, July 20, 2007, and subsequent amendments.

106 "Comments and Observations of the Office of Legal Affairs on the Draft Articles on Responsibility of International Organizations Adopted by the International Law Commission on First Reading in 2009," February 2011, UN Doc. A/CN.4/637/Add.1, 10 and 16. For a different view see Stefano Dorigo, "Imputazione e responsabilità internazionale per l'attività delle forze di *peace-keeping* delle Nazioni Unite," *Rivista di diritto internazionale* 85 (2002): 903.

(and possibly by third States) to the organization is indeed followed by the transfer of command and control powers over the respective military contingents. Accordingly, it may be assumed *a priori* that the conduct of the organs seconded exclusively to the organization will be attributed to the latter until the organization loses control over the military contingents seconded to it.[107]

The situation now described does not rule out the possibility, however, of attributing a wrongful conduct exclusively to the contributing State or to both the contributing State and the organization. Moreover, given that the contributing States may continue to exercise a certain degree of control over the troops placed at the organization's disposal, it is also possible for States both to exercise full control over the seconded troops, thus reactivating the national chain of command, and to influence the actual conduct of field operations without altering the EU chain of command. Indeed, as noted earlier, the States contributing military contingents participate in varying ways at different stages of decision making, both at the outset, by placing national caveats, and later in the course of the operations.[108] On the one hand, this circumstance does not mean that the organization loses 'ownership' of the operation; on the other hand, however, it enables States to influence the conduct of their respective contingents to some degree.[109]

In concrete terms, this means that where a contributing State resorts to the revert-back option,[110] thus breaking the EU chain of command, the State, rather than the organization, will be considered to exercise effective control over conduct; accordingly, any wrongful conduct will be attributed exclusively to that State. Furthermore, the attribution of conduct both to the organization and the contributing State cannot be ruled out *a priori* where the role of the latter in the decision-making process may have had a bearing on the wrongful conduct.[111]

---

107 Cf., *mutatis mutandis*, Cedric Ryngaert, "Apportioning Responsibility between the UN and Member States in UN Peace-Support Operations: An Inquiry into the Application of the 'Effective Control' Standard after *Behrami*," *Israel Law Review* 45 (2012), 160; Marten Coenraad Zwanenburg, *Accountability of Peace-Support Operations* (Leiden: Nijhoff, 2005), 37.

108 See above, Part I, para. 2.

109 See, among others, Christopher Leck, "International Responsibility in United Nations Peacekeeping Operations: Command and Control Arrangements and the Attribution of Conduct," *Melbourne Journal of International Law* 10 (2009): 346.

110 Again see above, Part I, para. 2.

111 Gaja, "Second Report," paras. 6–7 and 31. See also Giorgio Gaja, "Responsabilité des Etats et/ou des organisations internationales en cas de violations des droits de l'homme," in *La soumission des organisations internationales aux normes internationales relatives aux droits de l'homme: journée d'études de Strasbourg* (Paris: Pedone, 2009), 10.

It is true that on various occasions the EU has assumed the existence of a special regime of a customary nature applicable to regional economic integration organizations.[112] In particular, the EU considers itself bound by special rules in respect of responsibility for matters under its exclusive jurisdiction by virtue of the regulatory control that the organization exercises over Member States when the latter implement EU-imposed measures.[113] On the other hand, Article 64 DARIO allows a departure from the general regime of responsibility—and attribution of conduct—based on the rules of the organization and, in this case, the relationship between the EU and its Member States.

However, an exception on such grounds would not apply for military operations established by the EU, which do not fall within the scope of the exclusive competences attributed by its Member States.[114] The latter have not, in fact, relinquished control over security and defense to the EU. Even after the entry into force of the Treaty of Lisbon, the CSDP continued to follow an intergovernmental logic.[115]

However, special rules of attribution may also be found in other sources of international law: for example, Article 1(4) Draft Agreement on the Accession of the EU to the ECHR.[116] The comment regarding the provision clarifies that the rule should be interpreted as attributing (exclusively) to States the conducts engaged in by EU Member States both when they are implementing EU law and when they second organs to an international organization.[117] Article 3 Draft Agreement in any case recognized the possibility of considering the EU itself responsible, according to the co-respondent mechanism, which has enabled the EU to take part in proceedings before the Strasbourg Court as a defendant alongside Member States even where the conduct in question was not attributable to it.[118] However, as is well known, the Draft Agreement

---

112 See in this regard Pieter Jan Kuijper and Esa Paasivirta, "Does One Size Fit All? The European Community and the Responsibility of International Organizations," *Netherlands Yearbook of International Law* 36 (2005): 169.

113 Cf. "Responsibility of International Organizations. Comments and Observations Received from International Organizations," UN Doc. A/CN.4/545, 22.

114 See again Kuijper and Paasivirta, "EU International Responsibility," 51.

115 See generally Ugo Villani, "Gli sviluppi del Trattato di Lisbona in materia di politica estera e di sicurezza comune," *Studi sull'integrazione europea* 6 (2011): 17–18.

116 Cf. CoE, "Fifth Negotiation Meeting between the CDDH *Ad Hoc* Negotiation Group and the European Commission on the Accession of the European Union to the European Convention on Human Rights," Final Report to the CDDH, 47+1(2013)008Rev2, June 10, 2013, 5, Article 1, para. 4.

117 Ibid., 19, para. 23.

118 Cf. CoE, "Second Negotiation Meeting between the CDDH *Ad Hoc* Negotiation Group and the European Commission on the Accession of the European Union to the

did not receive the approval of the Court of Justice of the European Union (CJEU).[119] Consequently, at the present stage of development of international law, it seems problematic to affirm the existence of any special rule of this type in respect of the attribution of conduct—and, *a fortiori*, any special rule of a customary nature—which would be applicable in the case of military missions launched by the EU.[120]

The case of joint operations coordinated by Frontex is different. As we have said,[121] Frontex Operation *Themis* was established at the request of Italy and its operational plan was jointly adopted by the European Agency and the host State. Furthermore, by analyzing Frontex official information on the joint operation, it is possible to say that all the guest officers deployed within the framework of Operation *Themis* operate under the command and control of the host State and the Agency plays a mere role of coordination of national efforts. The responsibility of the host State is undisputed. All relevant documents stress, indeed, that both the EU's and the other Member States' intervention is intended to support and assist the actions put in place by the authorities of the host State, thus making it clear that the latter has the primary responsibility for ensuring compliance with all relevant instruments of international law when it comes to dealing with migration flows to its territory. This is hardly surprising, considering the fact that the ultimate responsibility of the Member States with regard to the maintenance of law and order and the safeguarding of internal security is expressly recognized by EU primary law, specifically by Articles 4(2) TEU and 72 TFEU. However, it does not seem possible to rule out *a priori* that a responsibility of other Member States, and of the EU, may also arise.

One might ask, then, which entity (or entities) should bear responsibility for any unlawful conduct committed in the context of Frontex Operation *Themis* by the guest officers taking part in the joint mission. The picture appears to be quite complex because Article 21(1) Regulation No. 2016/1624 establishes that the host State gives its instructions to all the guest officers in accordance

European Convention on Human Rights," September 17–19, 2012, Doc. 47+1(2012)R02, 2, para. 4. Regarding this issue, see generally Giorgio Gaja, "The Co-Respondent Mechanism According to the Draft Agreement for the Accession of the EU to the ECHR," *ESIL Reflections* 2, January 9, 2013, 3.

119 CJEU, opinion No. 2/13 of December 18, 2014. On the EU's accession to the ECHR, see broadly Ilaria Anrò, *L'adesione dell'Unione Europea alla CEDU. L'evoluzione dei sistemi di tutela dei diritti fondamentali in Europa* (Milan: Giuffrè, 2015).

120 For a different opinion see Andrea Spagnolo, *L'attribuzione delle condotte illecite nelle operazioni militari dell'Unione Europea* (Naples: Scientifica, 2016), 223.

121 See above, Part I, para. 3.

with the operational plan. Furthermore, Article 40(3) Regulation No. 2016/1624 states that the guest officers of Member States taking part in the joint operation "may only perform tasks and exercise powers under instructions from and, as a general rule, in the presence of border guards or staff (...) of the host Member State". Moreover, the use of force by guest officers may only be authorized with the consent of the home Member State and the host Member State, in the presence of border guards of the host Member State and in accordance with the latter's national law.[122] However, guest officers maintain some important links with the sending State. Thus, for instance, they must wear their own uniforms while performing their tasks;[123] they may carry weapons, ammunition, and equipment as authorized according to the home Member State's national law,[124] and the use of force, as already highlighted, must be authorized by the host State with the consent of the home State.[125]

In light of these elements, some legal commentators consider that the deployment of guest officers in Frontex joint operations may trigger a transfer of the attribution of conduct provided for by Article 6 DARSIWA,[126] which states that "the conduct of an organ placed at the disposal of a State by another State shall be considered an act of the former State under international law if the organ is acting in the exercise of elements of the governmental authority of the State at whose disposal it is placed."[127] It follows that the possibly of a transfer of attribution in light of Article 6 DARSIWA still retains its relevance, even if the effectiveness of such a transfer must be assessed on a case-by-case basis.[128] However, this does not rule out the possibility of invoking the responsibility of the sending State for failing to fulfill its due diligence obligation to prevent human rights violations.[129]

Other commentators, by contrast, relying on the fact that the sending home State maintains some control over its officers, argue that Article 17 DARSIWA

122 Cf. Article 40(6) Regulation No. 2016/1624.

123 Cf. Article 40(4) Regulation No. 2016/1624.

124 Cf. Article 40(5) Regulation No. 2016/1624.

125 Cf. again Article 40(6) Regulation No. 1624/2016.

126 Cf. Federico Casolari, "The EU's Hotspot Approach to Managing the Migration Crisis: A Blind Spot for International Responsibility?," *The Italian Yearbook of International Law* 25 (2015).

127 Cf. Article 6 DARSIWA.

128 See, in general terms, Giulio Bartolini, "Attribution of Conduct and Liability Issues Arising from International Disaster Relief Missions," *Vanderbilt Journal of Transnational Law* 48 (2015): 1041.

129 See ICJ, *Application of the Convention on the Prevention and Punishment of the Crime of Genocide (Bosnia and Herzegovina v Serbia and Montenegro)*, judgment of February 26, 2007, *ICJ Reports*, 2007, 43.

should be applied.[130] The provision deals with the case of a wrongful act of a State that is committed under the direction and control of a different State. In this case, both States are responsible for the wrongful act: the State giving instructions and the State receiving them.[131]

In both cases, however, it is necessary to assess, case by case, to which entities the wrongful act is ascribable. Only a case-by-case analysis may allow a proper attribution of conduct in the case of Frontex joint operations.[132]

Furthermore, in both cases, a shared responsibility of the States taking part in the joint Frontex Operation *Themis* and the EU could be established.[133] This possibility is not specifically foreseen either by the DARSIWA or DARIO adopted by the International Law Commission (ILC). However, the Special Rapporteur for the responsibility of international organizations pointed out that nothing prevents the possibility that a conduct may be attributed both to an organization and to another subject of international law.[134]

Part II. Applicable Law

1 *The Use of Force during Security Operations at Sea*

At this point of the discussion, we can analyze the primary rules applicable to all naval operations in the Central Mediterranean.

For the purpose of the so-called maritime security operations in international waters,[135] Resolution No. 2240 (2015) authorizes a certain use of force.[136]

130 Anna Liguori and Novella Ricciuti, "Frontex ed il rispetto dei diritti umani nelle operazioni congiunte alle frontiere esterne dell'Unione," *Diritti umani e diritto internazionale* 6 (2012): 555.

131 Cf. Commentary to Article 17 DARSIWA, para. 9.

132 For an in depth analysis cf. Melanie Fink, *Frontex and Human Rights: Responsibility in 'Multi-Actor Situations' under the ECHR and EU Public Liability Law* (Oxford: OUP, 2018).

133 On the subject of shared responsibility, as regards Frontex joint operations in general, see Maarten den Heijer, "Europe beyond its Borders: Refugee and Human Rights Protection in Extraterritorial Immigration Control," in *Extraterritorial Immigration Control. Legal Challenges*, ed. Bernard Ryan and Valsamis Mitsilegas (Leiden: Nijhoff, 2010), 192 and Efthymios Papastavridis, "'Fortress Europe' and Frontex: Within or without International Law?," *Nordic Journal of International Law* 79 (2010): 107.

134 Giorgio Gaja, "The Relations between the European Union and Its States from the Perspective of the ILC Articles on Responsibility of International Organizations," *SHARES Research Paper* 25 (2013), 2. On the issue see further below, Part V, para. 1.

135 See again stenographic record No. 18, 6.

136 Security Council Resolution No. 2240 (2015), para. 10.

The operations must in any case take place "in full compliance with international human rights law, as applicable."[137]

In this regard, since its decision in the *Saiga* case, the International Tribunal for the Law of the Sea (ITLOS) clarified that the use of force during law enforcement operations at sea is legitimate to the extent that is unavoidable, necessary and reasonable.[138] Analogous limitations are imposed, moreover, in general and conventional international law in relation to the right to life.[139] Thus, for instance, Article 2 ECHR forbids States to deprive someone of his or her life intentionally "unless it results from the use of force which is no more than absolutely necessary" (para. 2), in particular "in defence of any person from unlawful violence" (para. 2(a)) or "in order to effect a lawful arrest" (para. 2(b)).

The question is whether, in order to stop a vessel engaged in smuggling of migrants and/or trafficking of human beings, the officers involved in naval operations can simply fire at it, putting the lives of the people on board at risk or, on the contrary, should take all steps in order to avoid unnecessary harm. The ECtHR's case law on the use of lethal force is very clear in this respect: in the case of *McCann et al. v The United Kingdom*,[140] the Court considered that deprivations of life must be subject to the most careful scrutiny, particularly where deliberate lethal force is used, taking into consideration not only the actions of the agents of the State who actually administer the force but all the circumstances of the specific case, including the planning and control of the operation.[141]

In accordance with this landmark judgment, in smuggling and trafficking cases the use of lethal force would be permissible if armed traffickers and

137 Ibid.

138 ITLOS, *The M/V 'Saiga' Case No. 2* (*Saint Vincent and The Grenadines v Guinea*), judgment of July 1, 1999, *ITLOS Reports 1999*, 10, para. 153. For a similar judgment, see also the Court of Arbitration, *Guyana v Suriname*, award of September 17, 2007, *Reports of International Arbitral Awards* 33, 1, para. 405; cf. Efthymios Papastavridis, "The Use of Force at Sea in the 21st Century: Some Reflections on the Proper Legal Framework(s)," *Journal of Territorial and Maritime Studies* 2 (2015): 119.

139 Cf. Code of Conduct for Law Enforcement Officials (UN General Assembly Resolution No. 34/169 (1979), December 17, 1979), UN Doc. A/RES/34/169, Article 3 and Basic Principles on the Use of Force and Firearms by Law Enforcement Officials, adopted during the UN Congress on the Prevention of Crime and the Treatment of Offenders, which took place in Cuba from August 27 to September 7, 1990.

140 ECtHR, GC, *McCann et al. v The United Kingdom*, Appl. No. 18984/91, judgment of September 27, 1995.

141 Ivi, paras. 201 and 213.

smugglers were fired at while shooting at migrants on board their own vessels or at civil or military personnel on board some vessel of national or EU naval operations engaged in counter-smuggling and counter-trafficking operations in the Central Mediterranean.[142] The ECtHR has accepted that in certain well-defined circumstances Article 2 ECHR may also imply a positive obligation on the authorities to adopt preventive operational measures to protect the lives of those under their jurisdiction,[143] even in the event that their lives are at risk from the criminal acts of other individuals,[144] and also to investigate and repress violations of the right to life.[145]

More precisely, law enforcement measures at sea must be identified based on the priority assigned to the safety of the people aboard boats and must also avoid causing any damage to the marine environment or risk for the safety of navigation.[146]

In principle, therefore, measures adopted with the consent of the flag State and coercive measures against vessels employed in prohibited activities are tolerated.[147] However, the use of force should be allowed only in exceptional circumstances.[148] The need to ensure a correct application of the principles of necessity and proportionality, as well as elementary considerations of humanity,[149] lead us to conclude that such operations at sea should essentially admit the use of force only on grounds of self-defense of the individual,[150] including the case of a defensive action in favor of a third individual. More problematic is establishing whether the use of force could be admitted for

---

142 For similar conclusions as regards the use of force in the context of counter-piracy operations conducted in the Indian Ocean see Stefano Piedimonte Bodini, "Fighting Maritime Piracy under the European Convention on Human Rights," *European Journal of International Law* 22 (2011): 837.

143 See ECtHR, GC, *Osman v The United Kingdom*, Appl. No. 23452/94, judgment of October 28, 1998, paras. 115–116 and Human Rights Committee, *Baboeram-Adhin et al. v Suriname*, Communications Nos. 146/1983 and 148–154/1983, Decision of April 10, 1984; I-ACtHR, *Velásquez Rodríguez v Honduras*, judgment of July 29, 1988.

144 See ECtHR, *Maiorano et al. v Italy*, Appl. No. 28634/06, judgment of December 15, 2009; *Opuz v Turkey*, Appl. No. 33401/02, judgment of June 9, 2009; *Rantsev v Cyprus and Russia*, Appl. No. 25965/04, judgment of January 7, 2010.

145 On this issue see further above, Part II, para. 3.

146 See again Resolution No. 2240 (2015), para. 10 and Article 225 UNCLOS.

147 See also the declaration of the United Kingdom following the adoption of the Resolution No. 2240 (2015): UN Doc. S/PV.7531, October 9, 2015, 2.

148 Cf. Efthymios Papastavridis, "EUNAVFOR MED Operation Sophia: Fighting Smuggling of Migrants or Protecting Human Rights?," in *Protecting Human Rights in the European Union's External Relations*, ed. Sara Poli (The Hague: Cleer, 2016), 149–151.

149 See again ITLOS, *The M/V 'Saiga' Case No. 2*, para. 155.

150 See again stenographic record No. 18, 23.

the arrest of alleged smugglers. As stated by the ECtHR in the *Nachova* case, force ceases to be 'absolutely necessary' where it is known that the person to be arrested poses no threat to life or limb and is not suspected of having committed a violent offence.[151] In this case, law enforcement officers are prevented from putting the suspects' life at risk, even if this may result in the failure to arrest a fugitive.[152] *A fortiori*, the right to life of innocent people on board the intercepted vessel should receive a greater deal of protection: this is precisely the case with counter-smuggling and counter-trafficking operations where the use of force against the intercepted vessel is in principle precluded as long as migrants remain on board together with the smugglers.[153]

In any case, the specific conditions under which the operations take place require the adoption of suitable precautions in order to prevent panic from spreading aboard the overcrowded vessels, as this might severely prejudice both the life and physical integrity of the people on board and the safety of navigation.[154] Moreover, every law enforcement action at sea is subject to compliance with international obligations to safeguard life at sea and guarantee safe conditions for navigation.

2 *The Extra-Territorial Application of Human Rights*

All of the people intercepted or rescued at sea during the operations in the Mediterranean are entitled to several fundamental human rights. The relevance of the rules concerning the protection of human rights during law enforcement operations at sea does not appear to be under dispute.[155] In addition, the extraterritorial application of treaties on human rights whose scope of application is expressly limited to violations committed by a State party "within its jurisdiction"[156] is by now generally accepted both with respect to

151 Cf. ECtHR, GC, *Nachova et al. v Bulgaria*, Appl. Nos. 43577/98 and 43579/98, judgment of July 6, 2005, para. 107.

152 Cf. ECtHR, *Alikaj et al. v Italy*, Appl. No. 47357/08, judgment of March 29, 2011, para. 63.

153 Efthymios Papastavridis, *The Interception of Vessels on the High Seas: Contemporary Challenges to the Legal Order of the Oceans* (Oxford: Hart, 2013), 301; Matteo Tondini, "The Use of Force in the Course of Maritime Law Enforcement Operations," *Journal on the Use of Force and International Law* 4 (2017): 266.

154 Efthymios Papastavridis, "EUNAVFOR Operation Sophia and the International Law of the Sea," *Maritime Safety and Security Law Journal* 2 (2016): 57.

155 See again Resolution No. 2240 (2015), para. 10.

156 According to human rights bodies' case law, jurisdiction is considered as the trigger for the application of the substantive provisions of human rights instruments. The notion of jurisdiction used to determine the scope of human rights obligations is based on the dual notion of *de jure* and *de facto* jurisdiction. This dual criterion for the determination of jurisdiction serves the purpose of avoiding a gap in protection in those situations where

territories under the effective control of a State party[157] and in the event that such control is exercised in a given maritime area.[158]

Moreover, a derogation from the principle of the exclusive jurisdiction of the flag State over ships sailing on the high seas is justified when the State concerned consents to law enforcement operations carried out at sea and enables third States to draw the vessel into their area of effective control. Consequently, the flag State or State where a vessel is registered and international organizations taking part in naval operations off the Libyan coasts share the responsibility for protecting the human rights of the people aboard boats undergoing inspections and subjected to law enforcement operations on the high seas. Every State must comply not only with customary international law on human rights, but also its obligations under the human rights treaties it is party to.[159]

Human rights obligations arising from customary law and treaties are applicable indistinctly to migrants and the alleged smugglers captured during operations on the high seas. Both the former and the latter are in fact subject to the jurisdiction of the State that has seized the vessel in the event of detention, either aboard the ship from which the seizure was carried out[160] or on the vessel used for the prohibited activity, until the latter is fully under the effective and continuous control of the intercepting State.[161]

---

the State takes action outside a legal framework with the aim of avoiding the applicability of human rights treaties: in the literature, see Pasquale De Sena, *La nozione di giurisdizione statale nei trattati sui diritti dell'uomo* (Turin: Giappichelli, 2002) and Papanicolopulu, *International Law*, 118–119. Cf. also ECHR, Article 1; UN International Covenant on Civil and Political Rights (CCPR), adopted by the UN General Assembly on December 16, 1966, in force since March 23, 1976, *UNTS* vol. 999, 171, Article 2.

157 Cf., e.g., ECtHR, *Loizidou v Turkey*, Appl. No. 15318/89, judgment of March 23, 1995, para. 62; HRC, General Comment No. 31, The Nature of the General Legal Obligation Imposed on States Parties to the Covenant, May 26, 2004, UN Doc. CCPR/C/21/Rev.1/Add.13, para. 10; Committee against Torture, Conclusions and Recommendations: United Kingdom, November 18, 2004, Doc. CAT/C/CR/33/3, para. 4(b).

158 Cf. Greiβ and Petrig, *Piracy*, 108.

159 Cf., *mutatis mutandis*, ECtHR, *Ilaşcu et al. v Moldavia and Russia*, Appl. No. 48787/99, judgment of July 8, 2004, para. 322.

160 Cf., *mutatis mutandis*, ECtHR, GC, *Hirsi Jamaa et al. v Italy*, Appl. No. 27765/09, judgment of February 23, 2012. More will be said on this issue below, Part II, para. 3.

161 Cf., *mutatis mutandis*, ECtHR, *Medvedyev et al. v France*, Appl. No. 3394/03, judgment of March 29, 2010, para. 67. On the application of human rights in maritime operations see Efthymios Papastavridis, "European Convention of Human Rights and the Law of the Sea: The Strasbourg Court in Unchartered Waters?," in *The Interpretation and Application of the European Convention of Human Rights: Legal and Practical Implications*, eds. Malgosia Fitzmaurice and Panos Merkouris (Leiden: Nijhoff, 2013), 117 and Tullio Treves, "Human Rights and the Law of the Sea," *Berkeley Journal of International Law* 28 (2010): 1.

Should the Security Council extend the scope of its authorization to Libya's territorial waters, inland waters and territory,[162] moreover, we would logically expect it to confirm the relevance of human rights obligations during the operations in question, as well as the obligation to observe the applicable international humanitarian law. After all, the Libyan Unity Government is still engaged in an armed conflict of a non-international character against some pockets of resistance:[163] therefore, any States taking part in operations on Libyan territory should carefully formulate their respective operational rules of engagement (ROE) in such a way as to clearly distinguish law enforcement operations targeting migrant smugglers and traffickers from military operations against rebels. A similar concern was also expressed in the resolution whereby the Security Council authorized the operations against piracy on Somali territory.[164] Migrant smugglers and traffickers may no doubt be arrested and tried for their criminal activities, but they do not—as a rule—constitute legitimate military targets unless they actively take part in the hostilities.[165]

3 *The Obligation to Rescue People in Danger at Sea and the Right to Life*

It is now worth examining the content of the main primary norms that all members of the international community—including the EU and its Member States—must observe during naval operations in the Central Mediterranean. On the one hand, the traditional obligations under the law of the sea come into play, in particular the obligation to guarantee assistance to people in danger at sea. Also of relevance, on the other hand, are the general obligations established under treaties and laws on fundamental human rights, which must be observed by EU bodies as well when exercising the functions assigned to them and are applicable on an extraterritorial basis.[166]

---

162 See above, Part I, para. 1.

163 See above, Introduction.

164 Cf. Security Council Resolution No. 1851 (2008), November 10, 2008, para. 6; see in this regard Frederic Wiesenbach, "Uncertainty on Somalia's Beaches. The Legal Regime of Onshore Anti-Piracy Operations," *Journal of Conflict and Security Law* 19 (2014): 85.

165 Cf. International Committee of the Red Cross, "Interpretative Guidance on the Notion of Direct Participation in Hostilities under International Humanitarian Law," 2009, 41. Part of the illicit proceeds from activities carried out by people smugglers is used to finance the activities of rebels and terrorists in North Africa: cf. Natalino Ronzitti, "Libia, raid americani e titubanze italiane," *Affari Internazionali*, August 9, 2016. However, that is not sufficient to qualify smugglers as civilians taking part directly in the hostilities.

166 See above, Part II, para. 2. Regarding the extraterritorial application of the law of the EU, see generally Violeta Moreno-Lax and Cathryn Costello, "The Extraterritorial Application of the EU Charter of Fundamental Rights: From Territoriality to Facticity.

The obligation to provide assistance to every person "found at sea in danger of being lost" is one of the longest-standing rules of the law of the sea, by now a broadly recognized principle of customary law.[167] The content of primary laws is laid down in some international conventions codifying the rule, including the 1982 UNCLOS,[168] the 1974 Convention for the Safety of Life at Sea (SOLAS Convention),[169] the 1979 Convention on Maritime Search and Rescue (SAR Convention),[170] and the 1989 Convention on Salvage.[171]

More precisely, there is a specific obligation for all States to assist people in danger at sea using their flag vessels; this obligation applies to vessels in all maritime zones,[172] both to military and other State-owned vessels and to private vessels. It applies to all persons in distress, without distinction:[173] the nationality of the vessels or of the persons, their legal status and the activity in which they are engaged are irrelevant.[174] Thus, for instance, the fact that the persons to be saved are irregular migrants should not in any way hinder their right to be saved[175] and the same still holds true even when the persons to be

---

The Effectiveness Model," in *The EU Charter of Fundamental Rights: A Commentary*, ed. Steve Peers *et al.* (Oxford: Hart, 2014), 1663 and 1679.

167 Cf., among others, Richard Barnes, "Refugee Law at Sea," *International and Comparative Law Quarterly* 53 (2004): 49 and Seline Trevisanut, "Search and Rescue Operations in the Mediterranean: Factor of Cooperation or Conflict?," *International Journal of Marine and Coastal Law* 25 (2010): 523.

168 Article 98(1) UNCLOS.

169 International Convention for the Safety of Life at Sea, London, November 1, 1974, entered into force on May 25, 1980, *UNTS* vol. 1184, 278, and subsequent amendments, Annex, Chapter V, rule 33(1). The EU is not a party to the Convention, but the majority of its States Members have ratified it, with the exception of Austria, the Czech Republic and Hungary. All Parties accepted the amendments of 2004, in force since 2006, with the exception of Malta.

170 International Convention on Maritime Search and Rescue, Hamburg, April 27, 1979, entered into force on June 22, 1985, *UNTS* vol. 1405, 119 and subsequently amended in 1998 and 2004, Annex, para. 2.1.10. The EU is not a party to the Convention, but the majority of its States Members have ratified it without reservations, with the exception of Austria, the Czech Republic and Slovakia. All Parties accepted the amendments of 2004, with the exception of Malta.

171 International Convention on Salvage, London, April 28, 1989, entered into force on July 14, 1996, *UNTS* vol. 1953, 193, Article 10.

172 In the literature see, e.g., Irini Papanicolopulu, "The Duty to Rescue at Sea, in Peacetime and in War: A General Overview," *International Review of the Red Cross* 98 (2016): 495.

173 Cf. SAR Convention, Chapter 2.1.10 and SOLAS Convention, Rule 33.1.

174 Cf., among others, Richard Barnes, "The International Law of the Sea and Migration Control," in *Extraterritorial Immigration Control: Legal Challenges*, eds. Bernard Ryan and Valsamis Mitsilegas (Leiden: Nijhoff, 2010), 134.

175 Cf. "Interim Measures for Combating Unsafe Practices Associated with the Trafficking or Transport of Migrants by Sea," IMO Doc. MSC/Circ.896/Rev.1, June 12, 2001.

rescued are engaged in an unlawful activity. Confirmation of this may be found in the bilateral and multilateral conventions aimed at repressing wrongful conduct at sea.[176] Emblematic in this regard is Article 9(1)(a) Smuggling Protocol, which expressly mentions the obligation to ensure the safety and humane treatment of all people aboard vessels used for illegal smuggling of migrants. Any discrimination would be contrary to applicable law.[177]

Instances in which warships and State vessels do not comply with their duty to save life at sea will give rise to international responsibility of the State. Furthermore, while during wartime a warship may be excused from complying with the duty to rescue if it is involved in an engagement,[178] during peacetime no such exception can be found. The only exception to the duty to rescue life at sea, as provided in the UNCLOS, is the necessity not to endanger the rescuing vessel, its crew and its passengers (Article 98(1)). The SOLAS Convention, however, admits other grounds for not going to the rescue of a ship in distress.[179] The first concerns cases in which a ship is objectively 'unable' to provide rescue, for instance, due to the weather conditions, or the conditions of the vessel. The second concerns cases in which it is 'unreasonable' to expect the vessel to proceed to the rescue; that is, it might be objectively possible to go to the rescue but, in light of the actual circumstances of the vessels involved and the weather conditions, it would be unreasonable to expect the master of the requested vessel to undertake the rescue operation. Finally, the third exception concerns cases in which it is 'unnecessary' for a vessel to proceed to the rescue. This might be either because another vessel, which is closer, has already taken steps to fulfil the duty to rescue, or because the distance between the rescuing vessel and the endangered vessel is such that the former would not reach the latter in time. Commercial considerations should not play any role in the determination of the capacity of the vessel to rescue persons in distress at sea.[180]

Once persons in distress are saved, there are two duties incumbent upon the master of the ship which has saved them: to treat these people humanely, in

176 Cf. Article 5(4) of the Treaty between Italy and Spain for the repression of illegal drug trafficking at sea, Madrid, March 23, 1990 and Article 2 of the Protocol between Albania and Italy, April 2, 1997, implementing the terms pursuant to the exchange of letters of March 25, 1997. Cf. Tullio Scovazzi, "La tutela della vita umana in mare, con particolare riferimento agli immigrati clandestini diretti verso l'Italia," *Rivista di diritto internazionale* 88 (2005): 108.

177 See Papanicolopulu, "The Duty," 495.

178 Ivi, 504.

179 Cf. rule 33.1 SOLAS Convention.

180 See, e.g., Martin Davies, "Obligations and Implications for Ships Encountering Persons in Need of Assistance at Sea," *Pacific Rim Law and Policy Journal* 12 (2003): 109.

conformity with obligations arising under human rights treaties[181]—also taking into account the practical limitations encountered on board vessels, such as lack of space and the need to avoid the spread of disease[182]—and to deliver these people to a 'place of safety'.

The coastal State must further promote the establishment and operation of an adequate and effective maritime SAR system, also by entering into regional cooperation agreements between States.[183] The obligation to provide assistance extends to the disembarkation of the rescued persons in a 'place of safety', after which the operations may be considered to have concluded.[184] However, it is up to the State in whose SAR zone the rescue operations were carried out to ensure that the rescued persons are led to a safe place.[185] While a ship may temporarily be considered a place of safety, the people saved will eventually have to be disembarked on dry land. There are a number of options concerning disembarkation; however, it may be difficult to find a State that will allow the rescuing vessel to disembark rescued people in its ports, in particular if these people are likely to apply for asylum within that State. Two general principles regulate disembarkation: the first one provides that there is no right of entry into a State's ports; accordingly, a vessel that wants to disembark people rescued at sea into the ports of a State must have the consent of that State,[186] unless the vessel is in distress.[187] The second one is the *non-refoulement* principle.[188]

When the rescuing vessel has to deliver migrants and asylum seekers to a State, a dispute may arise as to which State that should accept these people, as States are often unwilling to assume their responsibilities and may prefer to close their ports to rescuing vessels. This is what occurred in the case of the *Tampa* incident in 2001 when Australia refused to accept 433 asylum seekers rescued by a Norwegian vessel in international waters, within Indonesia's

---

181 Cf. IMO Maritime Safety Committee, Resolution No. 167(78), "Guidelines on the Treatment of Persons Rescued at Sea," IMO Doc. MSC 78/26/Add.2, May 20, 2004 (IMO Rescue Guidelines), para. 5.1.2.

182 Cf. Rule 33.6 SOLAS Convention.

183 Cf. Article 98(2) UNCLOS and Chapter 3, Article 3.1.1 SAR Convention; on this issue see Trevisanut, "Search and Rescue," 523.

184 Cf. again IMO Rescue Guidelines. For a critical assessment of the guidelines, see generally Martin Ratcovich, "The Concept of 'Place of Safety': Yet Another Self-Contained Maritime Rule or a Sustainable Solution to the Ever-Controversial Question of Where to Disembark Migrants Rescued at Sea," *Australian Yearbook of International Law* 33 (2016): 81.

185 See again IMO Rescue Guidelines, principle 2.5.

186 Barnes, "The International Law," 118.

187 See further below, Part IV, para. 4.

188 Cf. IMO Rescue Guidelines, principle 6.17. See further below, Part II, para. 4.

SAR zone, but just 140 km from the Australian territory of Christmas Island.[189] A similar issue, however, arose more recently with the *Diciotti* case, when Italy, in 2018, refused for days to authorize the disembarkation of migrants on board the Italian-flagged ship and in several analogous cases.[190]

In 2004 the SAR Convention was amended to clarify the duties of States; however, the text does not answer the fundamental question as to which State the people rescued at sea should be disembarked in.[191] The State responsible for the SAR zone is given 'primary responsibility' for ensuring that assisted survivors are disembarked and delivered to a place of safety, taking into account the particular circumstances of the case. However, the text is silent as to what criteria should be applied in the event that no agreement is reached, and avoids clearly stating that, absent an agreement, the people saved should be disembarked in the State responsible for the SAR zone. Thus, it is not clear whether the State in whose SAR zone the rescue operations were carried out has a residual obligation to allow disembarkation on its own territory if it has been unable to locate a different place where disembarkation can take place safely,[192] or whether no such obligation is established.[193]

It is more problematic, however, to establish whether the rescue obligation has an interstate character,[194] or rather implies an actual right of those in danger at sea to be rescued.[195] Moreover, the provisions of human rights treaties oblige States not only to refrain from violating the right to life, but also to adopt appropriate measures to safeguard the life of anyone who is within their respective jurisdiction.[196] This means that there is a due diligence obligation, the

189 See, among others, Cecilia Baillet, "The Tampa Case and Its Impact on Burden Sharing at Sea," *Human Rights Quarterly* 25 (2003): 741.

190 See further below, Part IV, para. 4.

191 Cf. SAR Convention, Chapter 3.1.9 and SOLAS Convention, revised Rule 4.1.1. See Patricia Mallia, *Migrant Smuggling by Sea. Combating a Current Threat to Maritime Security through the Creation of a Cooperative Framework* (Leiden: Nijhoff, 2010), 100–101.

192 Cf. Seline Trevisanut, "Is There a Right to Be Rescued at Sea? A Constructive View," *Questions of International Law, Zoom-in* 4 (2014): 7.

193 In this sense cf. Daniel Ghezelbash *et al.*, "Securitization of Search and Rescue at Sea: The Response to Boat Migration in the Mediterranean and Offshore Australia," *International and Comparative Law Quarterly* 67 (2018): 322 and Violeta Moreno-Lax, "Seeking Asylum in the Mediterranean: Against a Fragmentary Reading of EU Member States' Obligations Accruing at Sea," *International Journal of Refugee Law* 23 (2011): 174.

194 See Efthymios Papastavridis, "Is There a Right to Be Rescued at Sea? A Skeptical View," *Questions of International Law, Zoom-in* 4 (2014): 19.

195 See Trevisanut, "Is There a Right to Be Rescued at Sea?," 3 and 7 and Id., "Recognizing the Right to be Rescued at Sea," *Ocean Yearbook* 31 (2017): 139.

196 Commission on Human Rights, "Basic Principles and Guidelines on the Right to a Remedy and Reparation for Victims of Violations of International Human Rights and

substance of which may vary depending on the State's ability to achieve the results required under international rules.[197] The positive obligation also extends to maritime rescue activities where the authorities of a coastal State are informed of the situation of danger in which an individual finds himself within the SAR zone of that State.[198] In this case, the State concerned will have jurisdiction, albeit only to the extent necessary to guarantee the rescue operations; accordingly, the authorities of coastal State are generally obliged to provide—directly or indirectly—adequate rescue services.[199] Issues may still remain concerning the extension of States' jurisdiction in some limit-cases which would pose an excessive burden on the relevant State. Human rights tribunals seized with the issue might provide useful guidance to this respect.[200]

However, recognizing the functional jurisdiction of a State appears to be more problematic where the call for help regards individuals in danger on the high seas, outside its SAR zone.[201] Normally, it falls on the MRCC in whose SRR the incident takes place to take responsibility for the coordination of the rescue operation.[202] However, distress calls may also arrive at other MRCCs; if this is the case, the first MRCC contacted retains responsibility for responding to the distress call until it is clear that the MRCC covering the SRR, or any other appropriate MRCC, has been found to be willing and able to assume responsibility for coordination and has effectively done so.[203]

Although safeguarding the life of migrants at sea is not expressly included among the functions assigned to Operations *Themis* and *Sophia*, military craft engaged in operations in the Central Mediterranean are also required to

Humanitarian Law," January 18, 2000, UN Doc. E/CN.4/2000/62, Annex, Article 1. The provision reproduces those included in the principal treaties on human rights (cf. Article 2 CCPR; Article 1 ECHR and Article 1 ACHR, San José, November 22, 1969, in force since July 18, 1978, *UNTS* vol. 1144, 143); ECtHR, *Xhavara et al. v Italy and Albania*, Appl. No. 39473/98, judgment of January 11, 2001. Cf. Moreno-Lax, "Seeking Asylum," 193–194.

197 Regarding this notion, see generally Riccardo Pisillo Mazzeschi, 'Due diligence' *e responsabilità internazionale degli Stati* (Milan: Giuffrè, 1989). Cf. also HRC, General Comment No. 36 (2018) on Article 6 of the International Covenant on Civil and Political Rights, on the Right to Life, October 30, 2018, Doc. CCPR/C/GC/36, paras. 7, 18 and 21.

198 Cf., *mutatis mutandis*, ECtHR, *Furdik v Slovakia*, Appl. No. 42994/05, decision of December 2, 2008.

199 See in this regard Trevisanut, "Is There a Right to Be Rescued at Sea?," 9.

200 See below, Part IV, para. 2.

201 Ibid., 11–14.

202 SAR Convention, Chapter 3.

203 IMO Guidelines on the Treatment of Persons Rescued at Sea, para. 6.7.

comply with the customary obligation.[204] Vessels assigned to both operations are trained and equipped to conduct maritime rescue activities and, for this purpose, they operate under the coordination of the SAR area authorities.[205] On the other hand, people smugglers often rely on small wooden boats or rubber dinghies that are unfit for navigation. As a result, the forces assigned to EU operations *Themis* and *Sophia* also have to carry out traditional SAR activities which would otherwise be left up to Coast Guard vessels of the coastal States or private boats with the coordination of the Italian, Maltese or, more recently, Libyan SAR authorities.[206]

4 *The* Non-refoulement *Obligation*

As a matter of principle, it is the sovereign right of a State to decide who it will admit to its territory. The UN General Assembly has reaffirmed on numerous occasions that States have the "sovereign right to enact and implement migratory and border security measures."[207] Although according to Article 12(2) of the International Covenant on Civil and Political Rights (CCPR), everyone is "free to leave any country, including his own",[208] international human rights law does not recognize a corollary right to enter another State's territory. In respect of border control, however, individuals have a right not to be returned to some States where their rights may be endangered. In order to respect these rights, a State may be obliged to admit an individual to its territory. The underlying principle of *non-refoulement* governs the questions as to whether and to where a State may expel persons.[209]

204 Cf. Preamble of Resolution No. 2240 (2015), paras. 3 and 10, and Preamble of Decision 2015/778/CFSP, para. 6.

205 See in this regard Giorgia Bevilacqua, "Exploring the Ambiguity of Operation Sophia between Military and Search and Rescue Activities," in *The Future of the Law of the Sea. Bridging Gaps between National, Individual and Common Interests*, ed. Gemma Andreone (Heidelberg: Springer, 2017): 178–179 and Marcello Di Filippo, "Irregular Migration and Safeguard of Life at Sea," in *International Law of the Sea: Current Trends and Controversial Issues*, ed. Angela Del Vecchio (The Hague: Eleven Internat, 2014), 9.

206 See again stenographic record No. 18, 26. See further below, Part IV, para. 1.

207 GA Resolution No. 61/165, December 19, 2006, para. 7; see also UNHCR, "Executive Committee on the International Protection of Refugees," Conclusion No. 97 (LIV) 2003; ECtHR, *Amuur v France*, Appl. No. 19776/92, judgment of May 20, 1996, para. 41.

208 On this issue see, among others, Nora Markard, "The Right to Leave by Sea: Legal Limits on EU Migration Control by Third Countries," *European Journal of International Law* 27 (2016): 609.

209 Cf. Lehmann, "Rights," 741.

Both the flag State and the coastal State are obliged to respect the principle of *non-refoulement*, that is, they are prohibited from forcibly returning migrants to the country they have escaped from and where they might face persecution, torture or other cruel, inhuman or degrading treatment (*direct refoulement*) or sending them to a country which in turn might expel them to another where such a danger exists (*indirect refoulement*).[210]

The prohibition was first established with regard to asylum seekers in Article 33(1) 1951 Geneva Convention relating to the Status of Refugees.[211] The Convention gives rise to *erga omnes* obligations; consequently, the international protection determined by one State in relation to the refugee status of an individual must also be granted by the other States Parties.[212] Moreover, the rules agreed on in the 1951 Convention have the nature of a treaty regime,[213] in the sense that the international protection it determines for asylum seekers constitutes an objective set of rules that also apply to some degree for third States, as an exception to the principle of relativity of treaties.[214] The *non-refoulement* obligation is also reiterated in numerous human rights treaties[215] with the objective of ensuring that an individual's expulsion will not result in him or her being deprived of guarantees that are considered fundamental for the States Parties. The convergence towards an 'obligation of conduct'

210 See generally, among others, Elihu Lauterpacht and Daniel Bethlehem, "The Scope and Content of the Principle of *Non-Refoulement*," in *Refugee Protection in International Law*, ed. Feller *et al.* (Cambridge: CUP, 2003), 87. Cf. UNHCR, "Summary Conclusions on the Concept of Effective Protection in the Context of Secondary Movements of Refugees and Asylum-Seekers," Expert Roundtable, Lisbon, December 9–10, 2002, para. 15(c).

211 1951 Convention relating to the Status of Refugees, Geneva, July 28, 1951, in force since April 22, 1954, *UNTS* vol. 189, 137. Libya has not ratified the Convention; nonetheless, this State must observe the customary constraint in respect of the prohibition of expulsion.

212 Cf. UNHCR, Executive Committee on the International Protection of Refugees, "Conclusion No. 12 (XXIX), Extraterritorial Effect of the Determination of Refugee Status (1978)," 190 and 394; cf. Francesco Salerno, "L'obbligo internazionale di *non-refoulement* dei richiedenti asilo," *Diritti umani e diritto internazionale* 4 (2010): 488.

213 Cf. UNHCR, General Assembly, UN Doc. A/RES/64/127, December 18, 2009, para. 2; regarding the notion of 'treaty regime', see generally Francesco Salerno, "Treaties Establishing Objective Regimes," in *The Law of Treaties beyond the Vienna Convention*, ed. Enzo Cannizzaro (Oxford: OUP, 2011): 225.

214 See again Salerno, "L'obbligo," 489.

215 Cf., *inter alia*, UN General Assembly, Universal Declaration of Human Rights, December 10, 1948, UN Doc. A/RES/217(III), Article 14; UN General Assembly, Inhuman or Degrading Treatment or Punishment, December 10, 1984, in force since June 26, 1987, *UNTS* vol. 1465, 85, Article 3(1); Articles 6 and 7 CCPR; Article 3 ECHR and Article 22(8) ACHR.

for States[216] leads toward the affirmation of a unitary customary law,[217] of an imperative nature.[218]

The EU references the 1951 Convention in Article 78(1) TFEU and considers it "the cornerstone of the international legal regime for the protection of refugees";[219] the *non-refoulement* obligation is also included, moreover, in the Charter of Fundamental Rights of the European Union (CFREU)[220] and is undoubtedly applicable to the EU operations in the Central Mediterranean.[221]

A coastal State's refusal to allow a ship to enter its territorial waters does not, as a rule, constitute a violation of the *non-refoulement* principle. However, a violation is deemed to have occurred if the refusal *de facto* implies the return of individuals to a country where their life or personal integrity is threatened.[222] Consequently, a State's denial of access to its territorial waters does not violate *per se* the *non-refoulement* obligation in the absence of evidence proving the impossibility of identifying a different safe place for the disembarkation of migrants.[223] The Italian request to other EU coastal States to allow boats engaged in the Mediterranean to enter their respective national ports may be read in this light.[224]

---

216 Regarding this notion, see Rüdiger Wolfrum, "Obligation of Result Versus Obligation of Conduct: Some Thoughts about the Implementation of International Obligations," in *Looking to the Future: Essays on International Law in Honor of Michael Reisman*, ed. Mahnoush H. Arsanjani *et al.* (Leiden: Nijhoff, 2011).

217 See generally Guy Goodwin-Gill and Jane McAdam, *The Refugee in International Law* (3rd edn. Oxford: OUP, 2007), 345; Seline Trevisanut, "The Principle of *Non-Refoulement* at Sea and the Effectiveness of Asylum Protection," *Max Planck Yearbook of United Nations Law* 12 (2008): 215.

218 Jean Allain, "The *Jus Cogens* Nature of *Non-Refoulement*," *International Journal of Refugee Law* 13 (2001): 533; Rene Bruin and Kees Wouters, "Terrorism and the Non-Derogability of *Non-Refoulement*," *International Journal of Refugee Law* 15 (2003): 26.

219 CJEU, GC, case C-31/09, *Bolbol*, judgment of June 17, 2010, paras. 12 and 37.

220 Cf. Articles 4, 18 and 19 CFREU, *OJEU* C 202, 389. There is also secondary European legislation, which references the 1951 Geneva Convention with more advanced guarantees: Cf. Council Regulation (EC) 343/2003, February 18, 2003, *OJEU* L 50, 1 and Council Directive No. 2004/83/EC, April 29, 2004, *OJEU* L 304, 12.

221 Cf. Decision No. 2015/778/CFSP, Preamble and Graham Butler and Martin Ratcovich, "Operation Sophia in Uncharted Waters: European and International Law Challenges for the EU Naval Mission in the Mediterranean Sea," *Nordic Journal of International Law* 85 (2016): 252 and Roberta Mungianu, *Frontex and* Non-Refoulement*: The International Responsibility of the EU* (Cambridge: CUP, 2016).

222 Barnes, "Refugee Law," 126; Goodwin-Gill and McAdam, "The Refugee," 277.

223 See again Barnes, "Refugee Law," 126.

224 For an assessment of this issue see Pasquale De Sena and Francesca De Vittor, "La 'minaccia' italiana di 'bloccare' gli sbarchi di migranti e il diritto internazionale," *SIDI Blog*, July 1, 2017. More on this issue will be said below, Part IV, para. 4.

The customary core of the prohibition of *refoulement* implies negative obligations for a State in terms of conduct, in addition to several positive obligations for States Parties to the 1951 Convention to achieve certain results. Under the former, which constitutes the *jus cogens* part of this obligation, the State may not expel, transfer or extradite individuals who may be victims of torture or other violations of fundamental rights; positive obligations, by contrast, require the State to guarantee access to precise procedures for obtaining refugee status[225] or a complementary form of international protection.[226] Such obligations also apply in the case of mass exoduses[227] and rule out the possibility of the State invoking an exemption on grounds of necessity, at least in relation to the *jus cogens* part of the *non-refoulement* obligation.[228]

The application of the prohibition of *refoulement* in mainly territorial terms does not rule out its enforceability in every other area in which a State exercises jurisdiction, including maritime areas[229] such as territorial waters, the contiguous zone, and also the high seas during interdiction or maritime rescue operations.[230] The ECtHR established this in the *Hirsi* case in 2012,[231] where a group of irregular Somali and Eritrean migrants was intercepted on the high seas by the Italian Navy. The migrants were transferred onto Italian

225 See in this regard Reinhard Marx, "*Non-Refoulement*, Access to Procedures and Responsibility for Determining Refugee Claims," *International Journal of Refugee Law* 7 (1995): 393.

226 Cf. UNHCR, Executive Committee, "Conclusion No. 103 (LVI) On the Provision on International Protection Including through Complementary Forms of Protection (2005)"; in the literature, see generally Jane McAdam, *Complementary Protection in Refugee Law* (Oxford: OUP, 2005), 19.

227 Cf. UNHCR, Executive Committee, Conclusion No. 19 (XXXI) Temporary Refuge (1980) and No. 22 (XXXII) Protection of Asylum-Seekers in Situations of Large-Scale Influx (1981).

228 Cf. Articles 25 and 26 DARSIWA, *Yearbook of the International Law Commission*, 2001, vol. 2, No. 2, UN Doc. A/56/10 (2001).

229 Cf. UNHCR, "Advisory Opinion on the Extraterritorial Application of Non-Refoulement Obligations under the 1951 Convention relating to the Status of Refugees and Its 1967 Protocol," January 26, 2007, 13; Anja Klug and Tim Howe, "The Concept of State Jurisdiction and the Applicability of the *Non-Refoulement* Principle to Extraterritorial Interception Measures," in *Extraterritorial Immigration Control. Legal Challenges*, ed. Bernard Ryan and Valsamis Mitsilegas (Leiden: Nijhoff, 2010), 92.

230 See generally IACoHR, *Haitian Center for Human Rights et al. v United States*, case No. 10.675, report No. 51/96, March 13, 1997, Doc. OEA/Ser.L/V/II.95 Doc. 7 rev (1996), para. 163 and Lory Diana Rosenberg, "The Courts and Interception: The US Interdiction Experience and Its Impact on Refugees and Asylum Seekers," *Georgetown Immigration Law Journal* 17 (2003): 199.

231 See again ECtHR, GC, *Hirsi Jamaa et al.* For commentary see Mariagiulia Giuffrè, "Watered-Down Rights on the High Seas: Hirsi Jamaa and Others v Italy," *International Comparative Law Quarterly* 61 (2012): 728.

military vessels and taken back to Tripoli on the basis of bilateral agreements concluded with Libya in 2008.[232] The ECtHR judged that the Italian authorities had, among other things, violated Article 3 ECHR, as they had exposed the applicants to the concrete risk of being victims of inhuman and degrading treatments.[233] For one thing, the events had taken place entirely aboard vessels of the Italian armed forces and, in the period between the boarding of the vessel and transfer of its occupants to the Libyans, the applicants were under the full, continuous and exclusive control of the Italian authorities.[234] In addition, the treatment given to the illegal migrants taken back to Libya was attested by numerous reports produced by international bodies and non-governmental organizations (NGOs).[235]

Also in light of the above-mentioned case law, an intercepting State—or one engaged in maritime rescue operations—must always comply with the general and agreed obligation not to send back illegal immigrants who would otherwise see their fundamental rights violated. If the State is a party to the 1951 Convention, it must likewise assure that the procedures for the recognition of refugee status duly take place. In the case of States Parties to the 1951 Convention, it is thus legitimate to send back migrants only after verifying the reasons that have induced them to seek entry into the country and only if the rights of those seeking recognition of refugee status are respected.[236] For this purpose, a summary check must be carried out aboard the vessel to ascertain the identity of the person concerned[237] so as not to preclude *a priori* the

232 See above, Introduction. For some considerations on the agreement, see Chiara Favilli, "Quali modalità di conclusione degli accordi internazionali in materia di immigrazione," *Rivista di diritto internazionale* 88 (2005): 156 and Seline Trevisanut, "Immigrazione clandestina via mare e cooperazione fra Italia e Libia dal punto di vista del diritto del mare," *Diritti umani e diritto internazionale* 3 (2009): 611–615. On the push-back practice in the Mediterranean, see generally Francesca De Vittor, "Soccorso in mare e rimpatri in Libia: tra diritto del mare e tutela internazionale dei diritti dell'uomo," *Rivista di diritto internazionale* 92 (2009): 800.

233 ECtHR, GC, *Hirsi Jamaa et al.*, paras. 136 and 137.

234 Ibid., paras. 81–82. The same may be said also in cases where a private vessel flying a foreign flag is intercepted on the high seas and escorted to the port: again, see ECtHR, *Rigopoulos v Spain*, Appl. No. 37388/97, judgment of January 12, 1999; GC, *Medvedyev et al.*, paras. 66–67.

235 ECtHR, *Hirsi Jamaa et al.*, paras. 123 and 126.

236 Cf. UNHCR, Executive Committee, Conclusion No. 15 (XXX) Refugees without an Asylum Country (1979), para. b.

237 Regarding the presumptive character of this ascertainment, see Jean-François Durieux and Jane McAdam, "*Non-Refoulement* through Time. The Case for a Derogation Clause to the Refugee Convention in Mass Influx Emergencies," *International Journal of Refugee Law* 16 (2004): 12.

asylum seeker's access to the territory of the State and the initiation of the status recognition procedure.[238]

Some violations of the *non-refoulement* obligation may also occur during the EU operations in the Central Mediterranean. It is true that people intercepted and rescued at sea within the framework of operations *Themis* and *Sophia* are presently handed over to the Italian authorities.[239] However, SAR activities are not *per se* the responsibility of EU operations and they always take place under the direction of the rescue coordination centre of the State in whose SAR area the operations are conducted.[240] Consequently, it cannot be ruled out *a priori* that some activities might be coordinated by the centre of a State that does not provide every guarantee established by human rights law. For example, in the case of SAR operations implemented within the SAR area of Greece, disembarkation may take place within Greek territory, despite the serious structural deficiencies found in the reception and asylum system of that State.[241] More recently, the same issue has been affirmed with respect to Italy after the decision of the Italian Government to close its ports mainly to NGOs vessels engaged in SAR operations at sea and registered in third States or flying a foreign flag[242] and with respect to Libya after the institution of a Libyan SRR.[243]

A further problematic aspect when it comes to observance of the *non-refoulement* principle lies in the multifaceted efforts that the EU has been engaging in for some time to favor relations with North African countries and improve its control over its Mediterranean borders.[244] The EU's interest in this regard—as also attested by the deployment of the civilian mission EUBAM Libya[245]—is to help Libya to achieve more effective control over migrant flows in the land and sea areas subject to its exclusive jurisdiction; this objective is

238 Cf. Goodwin-Gill and McAdam, "The Refugee," 205.

239 In this regard, cf. broadly Bevilacqua, "Exploring," 181–183.

240 Cf. Trevisanut, "Search and Rescue," 524. See above, Part II, para. 3.

241 See generally ECtHR, GC, *M.S.S. v Belgium and Greece*, Appl. No. 30696/09, judgment of January 21, 2011, para. 137. For commentary see Laura Magi, "Protezione dei richiedenti asilo '*par ricochet*' o protezione '*par moitié*'?, La Grande Camera ripatisce fra gli Stati contraenti le responsabilità per violazioni della Convenzione europea conseguenti al trasferimento di un richiedente asilo in attuazione del regolamento Dublino II," *Rivista di diritto internazionale* 94 (2011): 824; cf. in this regard Papastavridis, "EUNAVFOR MED Operation Sophia," 152.

242 On the issue see below, Part IV, para. 4.

243 On the issue see below, Part IV, para. 1.

244 Cf., among others, Susan Kneebone, Christopher McDowell and Gareth Morrell, "A Mediterranean Solution? Chances of Success," *International Journal of Refugee Law* 18 (2006): 492.

245 The EUBAM Libya mission was established with Decision 2014/16/CFSP of the Political and Security Committee, January 14, 2014, *OJEU* L 14, 13, with the objective of providing support to the Libyan authorities and with a view to increasing, in the short term, the

also pursued through the conclusion of a series of agreements with several North African States such as Egypt, Algeria and Tunisia regarding the capture of people smugglers.[246] Moreover, within the framework of the CSDP, the EU can conclude agreements—without any constraints *ratione materiae*—on specific aspects of a single military operation.[247] Such agreements were concluded with third States that can hardly be regarded as a 'safe place', either in the light of the SOLAS and SAR Conventions or in terms of compliance with the *non-refoulement* principle.[248] However, such agreements are lawful exclusively to the extent in which they do not end up prejudicing the obligations of States Parties to the 1951 Geneva Convention.[249]

Analogous problems could also arise in the event that the EU decides to conclude agreements for the transfer of suspected smugglers and traffickers captured within the framework of the EU operations *Themis* and *Sophia* to Libya or other third States that manifest an intention of subjecting them to criminal prosecution.[250]

5 *Pre-Trial Detention of Alleged Smugglers*

From the perspective of compliance with fundamental human rights, the legitimacy of the arrest and detention measures adopted against alleged smugglers by the forces assigned to operations *Themis* and *Sophia* during law enforcement operations on the high seas appears to be a particularly problematic issue. Investigation into this aspect focuses on possible violations of the right to liberty and security of person established by Article 5 ECHR and Article 9 CCPR, among others. Excluded from the investigation are the aspects relating to the administrative detention of victims of trafficking or irregular people smuggling.[251]

---

security of the State's land, sea and air borders as well as implementing a broader long-term strategy for an integrated border management.

246 Analogous bilateral agreements were concluded by Spain with several North African States, including Morocco, Senegal, Mauritania and Cape Verde for joint patrols to be conducted by the Spanish Coast Guard and the border authorities of the States parties to the agreements with the aim of preventing migrant flows from the latter; see in this regard Paula Garcia Andrade, "Extraterritorial Strategies to Tackle Irregular Migration by Sea," in *Extraterritorial Immigration Control: Legal Challenges*, eds. Bernard Ryan and Valsamis Mitsilegas (Leiden: Nijhoff, 2010), 311. See further below, Part IV, para. 1.

247 See in this regard Naert, *International Law Aspects*, 122.

248 See in this regard Butler and Ratcovich, "Operation Sophia," 249.

249 Cf. Article 14 Smuggling Protocol and UNHCR, Executive Committee, Conclusion No. 97 (LIV), On Protection Safeguards in Interception Measures (2003).

250 See again Butler and Ratcovich, "Operation Sophia," 257. On this issue see further below, Part III, para. 3.

251 On this issue see generally Gallagher and David, *The International Law*, 599.

The notion of 'detention' of the vessel's captain and crew adopted by the ITLOS is rather broad.[252] It includes every measure designed to restrict an individual's freedom of movement and which may reach a certain degree irrespective of the *nomen iuris* attributed by individual States in the concrete case concerned.[253] A similar notion has also been adopted by the ECHR: in fact, it includes both detention following arrest or conviction by the judicial authorities of the State and various other forms of limitation of an individual's personal freedom.[254]

More precisely, Article 5 ECHR establishes a protection against every arbitrary deprivation of personal freedom. Specific restrictions on individual liberty are allowed solely in the cases and under the conditions set forth expressly in Article 5(1)(a)–(f): in particular, such restrictions can be adopted exclusively on the basis of a procedure prescribed by law and which is both accessible and predictable.[255] The right to personal liberty is also protected by a series of substantial and procedural guarantees enucleated in Article 5(2)–(5), including the right to have the question brought before a judge 'promptly'.[256]

The first problematic issue tied to the operations in the Mediterranean regards the possibility of predicting the adoption of detention measures and the detention measures themselves with any degree of certainty. Regarding this issue, the ECHR has affirmed on many occasions that "where deprivation of liberty is concerned, it is particularly important that the general principle of legal certainty be satisfied. It is therefore essential that the conditions for deprivation of liberty under domestic and/or international law be clearly defined and that the law itself be foreseeable in its application, so that it meets the standard of 'lawfulness' set by the Convention, a standard which requires that all law be sufficiently precise to avoid all risk of arbitrariness."[257]

---

252 See, for example, ITLOS, *'Camouco'* (*Panama v France*), judgment of February 7, 2000, *ITLOS Reports*, 2000, 10 and *'Monte Confurco'* (*Seychelles v France*), judgment of December 18, 2000, *ITLOS Reports*, 2000, 86.

253 Cf. ITLOS, *'Camouco'*, para. 71 and *'Monte Confurco'*, para. 90. The difference between restrictions on the freedom of movement which arrive at such a point as to be considered deprivation of liberty pursuant to Article 5(1) ECHR and restrictions falling under Article 2 Protocol No. 4 is the degree or severity of the restriction, not its nature: cf., among others, ECtHR, *Guzzardi v Italy*, Appl. No. 7367/76, judgment of November 6, 1980, para. 93; *Rantsev v Cyprus and Russia*, Appl. No. 25965/04, judgment of January 7, 2010, para. 314.

254 Cf. ECtHR, *Guzzardi v Italy*, para. 95.

255 Cf., *inter alia*, ECtHR, GC, *Del Río Prada v Spain*, Appl. No. 42750/09, judgment of October 21, 2013, para. 125; GC, *Creangă v Romania*, Appl. No. 29226/03, judgment of February 23, 2012, para. 120.

256 See in particular Article 5(3) ECHR.

257 See generally, among others, ECtHR, *Malone v The United Kingdom*, Appl. No. 8691/79, judgment of August 2, 1984, para. 67; *Baranowski v Poland*, Appl. No. 28358/95, judgment of March 28, 2000, paras. 50–52.

The same guarantees also apply in the case of interdiction and prevention detention activities at sea.[258] The *Medvedyev* case is emblematic in this regard.[259] On June 13, 2002, a merchant ship named *Winner*, flying the Cambodian flag and suspected of being engaged in drug trafficking activity, was intercepted by the French Navy on the high seas of the Atlantic Ocean. The interdiction operation was made possible by virtue of the consent expressed by the flag State in a diplomatic note, dated June 7, 2002, which authorized France to intercept, inspect and adopt other measures against the ship.[260] The crew was detained aboard the *Winner* throughout the entire voyage to the French port of Brest, where the ship landed on June 26, 2002 and the alleged perpetrators were handed over to the local authorities so that criminal proceedings could be brought against them. The members of the crew of the *Winner* were ultimately convicted in France for drug trafficking and, after having used all internal means of appeal to no avail, they decided to submit an application to the ECtHR. Among other things, the applicants claimed that the French authorities had violated Article 5(1) ECHR by arbitrarily depriving them of their personal liberty: in the view of the applicants, the arrest and subsequent detention of the crew had no legal basis either in French or international law.[261]

In a judgment delivered on July 10, 2008, the Chamber highlighted the arbitrary character of the detention in that neither French law nor the diplomatic note contained any provisions regulating the conditions of deprivation of personal liberty on board the ship or, in particular, allowing the possibility of contacting a lawyer or family members, and the absence of any judicial supervision over the pre-trial detention at sea.[262]

The issue was then brought before the Grand Chamber, whose analysis was essentially centred on two questions: whether it was possible to find a clear

258 Cf. ECtHR, GC, *Medvedyev et al.*, para. 80.

259 ECtHR, *Medvedyev et al.*, Appl. No. 3394/03, judgment of July 10, 2008, confirmed by the Grand Chamber in the judgment of March 29, 2010. For commentary see Douglas Guilfoyle, "*Medvedyev and Others v. France*, European Court of Human Rights," *International Journal of Marine and Coastal Law* 25 (2010): 437; Efthymios Papastavridis, "European Court of Human Rights Medvedyev and Others v. France (Grand Chamber, Application No. 3394/03) Judgment of 29 March 2010," *International and Comparative Law Quarterly* 59 (2010): 867.

260 Para. 10 of the diplomatic note stated: "the Ministry of Foreign Affairs and International Cooperation ... has the honour formally to confirm that the royal government of Cambodia authorizes the French authorities to intercept, inspect and take legal action against the ship *Winner*, flying the Cambodian flag XUDJ3, belonging to 'Sherlock Marine' in the Marshall Islands".

261 ECtHR, GC, *Medvedyev et al.*, para. 43. Regarding this case, see broadly Treves, "Human Rights," 8.

262 ECtHR, *Medvedyev et al.*, para. 61. Analogous concerns also emerge in the individual opinion of the judge Berro-Lefèvre, echoed by the judges Lorenzen and Lazarova Trajkovska.

legal basis for the French action and whether it was such as to fulfil the accessibility and foreseeability requirements laid down by the Convention.[263] The Grand Chamber pointed out first of all that the lawfulness of the detention had to be assessed in reference to national law but, where appropriate, reference could also be made to other legal standards, including those established by international law.[264] At the time the events took place, French domestic legislation pertaining to interdiction at sea for drug trafficking was exclusively aimed at transposing the obligations undertaken by France as a party to the 1988 UN Convention against Illicit Traffic in Narcotic Drugs and Psychotropic Substances,[265] which Cambodia itself was not a party to.[266] Nor was Cambodia a party to the UNCLOS; consequently, the only legal basis for France's action was to be found in the exchange of diplomatic notes between the two States.

Although, in the Court's opinion, the diplomatic note might effectively justify France's interdiction operation, it was not sufficiently clear about the possibility of limiting the personal liberty of the crew.[267] A further problem was the circumstance that the diplomatic note could not be considered to have met the accessibility and foreseeability requirements established by the Convention. Indeed, it was an *ad hoc* agreement adopted in the absence of any multilateral or bilateral treaty. And this circumstance was proof of the singular nature of the cooperation measure adopted in the case concerned.[268] Consequently, the Court ultimately recognized France's violation of Article 5(1) ECHR: the deprivation of personal liberty to which the applicants had been subjected between the boarding of the *Winner* and its arrival in the French port of Brest could not be considered lawful, according to the parameters established by the Convention, due to the absence of a legal basis such as to satisfy the certainty, accessibility and foreseeability requirements.[269]

Analogous considerations could also be put forward in relation to the ongoing multilateral operations in the Central Mediterranean and, as regards the specific issues of interest here, within the framework of operations *Themis* and *Sophia*. To begin with, Decision No. 2015/778—unlike the decision establishing

263 ECtHR, GC, *Medvedyev et al.*, paras. 82–103.

264 Ibid., para. 79; see also ECtHR, *Bozano v France*, Appl. No. 9990/82, judgment of December 18, 1986, para. 54; GC, *Assanidze v Georgia*, Appl. No. 71503/01, judgment of April 8, 2004, para. 171; GC, *McKay v The United Kingdom*, Appl. No. 543/03, judgment of October 3, 2006, para. 30.

265 UN Convention against Illicit Traffic in Narcotic Drugs and Psychotropic Substances, Vienna, December 20, 1988, in force since November 11, 1990, *UNTS* vol. 1582, 95.

266 ECtHR, GC, *Medvedyev et al.*, para. 90.

267 Ibid., para. 99.

268 Ibid., para. 100.

269 Ibid., para. 102.

Operation *Atalanta*[270]—does not establish a clear mandate for the forces engaged in the operation to assure the arrest, detention and criminal prosecution of suspected smugglers.[271] In the Preamble of the decision, it is provided that States may adopt "appropriate measures against the vessels, persons and cargo"[272] and it is further established that a State may take "appropriate measures against persons present on its territory whom it suspects of smuggling or trafficking humans with a view to their possible arrest and prosecution, in accordance with international law and its domestic law."[273]

Secondly, Security Council Resolution No. 2240 (2015) makes only generic reference, in the Preamble, to States' obligations under international law to exercise due diligence in their efforts to prevent and combat illegal migrant smuggling and human trafficking, including the obligation to investigate and punish perpetrators of unlawful conduct. Furthermore, in paragraph 15, the Council "calls upon all States with relevant jurisdiction under international law and national legislation, to investigate and prosecute persons responsible for acts of migrant smuggling and human trafficking at sea."

In both cases, however, exactly as in the Smuggling Protocol,[274] only the *enforcement jurisdiction*—which regards the possibility of adopting executive measures against a vessel—is established with certainty. The option for States to establish a geographical extension of criminal provisions for the unlawful conducts in question—so-called *prescriptive jurisdiction*—must, by contrast, be established on each occasion based on the pertinent rules of international law in respect of criminal jurisdiction or the internal legislation of each State.[275]

As a result, the indications provided thus far do not seem to constitute a sufficient legal basis for arrest and detention in light of the cited case law. The ECtHR has in fact clarified that indications of a similar kind do not comply

270 See again Decision No. 2008/851/CFSP, Article 2(e).

271 See again in this regard Butler and Ratcovich, "Operation Sophia," 254. Regarding the distinction between jurisdiction *in rem* and *in personam* see Efthymios Papastavridis, "Enforcement Jurisdiction in the Mediterranean Sea: Illicit Activities and the Rule of Law on the High Seas," *International Journal of Marine and Coastal Law* 25 (2010) 558. On the criminal prosecution of suspected smugglers see below, Part III.

272 Cf. Decision No. 2015/778/CFSP, Preamble, para. 7.

273 Ibid.

274 Cf. Article 8(7) Smuggling Protocol; Gallagher and David, *The International Law*, 244–246.

275 In this regard, see Robin Rolf Churcill and Alan Vaughan Lowe, *The Law of the Sea* (3rd edn. Manchester: Juris, 1999), 214 and Douglas Guilfoyle, *Shipping Interdiction and the Law of the Sea* (Cambridge: CUP, 2009), 17. Regarding the notions of *prescriptive jurisdiction* and *enforcement jurisdiction* see Frederick Alexander Mann, "The Doctrine of Jurisdiction in International Law," *Recueil des cours* (1964): 128 and Roger O'Keefe, "Universal Jurisdiction: Clarifying the basic concept," *Journal of International Criminal Justice* 2 (2004): 741.

with the parameter established by Article 5(1) ECHR. Moreover, they do not ensure adequate protection against possible arbitrary violations of the right to individual liberty, since they lack any provisions regulating the conditions of deprivation of liberty on board vessels or the possibility of enforcing the individual guarantees established to defend that right.

In the context outlined by the Court, there is thus a need for the individual States taking part in the maritime rescue and interdiction operations to provide clear, precise, predictable rules in their legislation concerning the specific conditions of arrest and pre-trial detention; such legislation should also provide for adequate procedural guarantees, including judicial supervision.[276] Otherwise, any detention of suspected smugglers during the naval activities conducted within the framework of Operation *Sophia* could be in violation of Article 5 ECHR. Analogous considerations apply, moreover, for the operations at sea coordinated by Frontex.[277]

A decisive consideration for determining whether the coercive measures adopted against alleged smugglers constitute a deprivation of liberty compatible with the standards established by human rights treaties regards the duration of the restrictive measure.[278]

Aspects related to the duration of measures that restrict personal freedom were specifically considered by the ECtHR in the *Rigopoulos* case.[279] On January 23, 1995, the *Archangelos*, a ship flying the Panamanian flag, suspected of transporting a substantial cargo of narcotic drugs, was boarded on the high seas of the Atlantic Ocean by the crew of a Spanish Navy vessel as it was sailing towards Europe. Both the boarding operations and subsequent seizure of the ship were carried out, with the flag State's consent, within the framework of a policy of cooperation among States aimed at combating drug trafficking and,

---

276 With regard to the detention of alleged pirates, see ECtHR, *Ali Samatar et al. v France*, Appl. Nos. 17110 and 17301, judgment of December 4, 2014 and *Hassan et al. v France*, Appl. Nos. 46695 and 54588, judgment of December 4, 2014.

277 See in this regard Moreno-Lax, "Seeking Asylum," 188–190. The European legislator had already in the past proposed that persons aboard ships with no nationality and considered to be engaged in migrant smuggling could be arrested: see Council Decision No. 2010/252, April 26, 2010, which supplements the Schengen Borders Code in relation to the surveillance of the sea external borders within the framework of the operational cooperation coordinated by the European Agency for the Management of Operational Cooperation at the External Borders of the Member States of the European Union, *OJEU* L 111, 20, Annex, Part I, paras. 2.5.2.5. and 2.4(d).

278 See in this regard Cornelis Wolfram Wouters and Maarten Den Heijer, "The Marine I Case: A Comment," *International Journal of Refugee Law* 22 (2010): 14–15.

279 ECtHR, *Rigopoulos v Spain*, Appl. No. 37388/97, decision of January 12, 1999.

more precisely, in accordance with the provisions of Articles 17(3) and 17(4) 1988 UN Convention against Illicit Traffic in Narcotic Drugs and Psychotropic Substances which, at the time of the events in question, was in force in both States.

Following the discovery of a large amount of cocaine on board the ship, the Spanish authorities decided to take the members of the crew into custody and transport them to the port of Las Palmas—where they arrived after a 16-day voyage—for the purpose of prosecuting them. Mr. Rigopoulos, after having attempted, in vain, all internal avenues of appeal, submitted an application to the ECtHR, complaining of a violation of Article 5(3) ECHR which establishes, among other things, that every person arrested or detained "shall be brought promptly before a judge or other officer authorized by law to exercise judicial power". The applicant complained, precisely, about the excessive length of the pre-trial detention on board the ship, during which his situation was not examined by the competent judicial authority.

In the Court's opinion, a period of 16 days between the crew's arrest and the time of the first contact with the competent judicial authority must—as a rule—be considered incompatible with the promptness requirement established by Article 5(3) ECHR.[280] The latter provision, read in combination with Article 5(1)(c), establishes a framework of minimum guarantees against all arbitrary limitations of individual liberty.[281]

However, in consideration of the particular conditions under which the maritime interdiction operations had taken place, the Court judged that a more 'flexible' approach should be taken. In the Court's opinion, in fact, the particular circumstances of the arrest—considered 'wholly exceptional'—made it materially impossible to bring the crew before the judicial authority any sooner, due to the distance to be travelled by sea.[282] Consequently, the Court found that there had been no violation of Article 5(3) ECHR: exceptional circumstances not ascribable to the intercepting State were thus considered sufficient to justify the lengthy duration of the detention imposed on the crew prior to prosecution.[283]

---

280 ECtHR, *Rigopoulos v Spain*, 9; for a similar interpretation, see also ECtHR, GC, *Medvedyev et al.*, para. 130.

281 Cf. Article 5(3) ECHR. Judicial control over an arrest may also be exercised at sea, through a videoconference.

282 ECtHR, *Rigopoulos v Spain*, paras. 9–10; for a similar interpretation, see also GC, *Medvedyev et al.*, paras. 131–134.

283 Again see ECtHR, *Rigopoulos v Spain*, para. 9; for a similar interpretation, see also GC, *Medvedyev et al.*, para. 130.

The limited dimensions of the Mediterranean basin do not seem *ictu oculi* sufficient grounds for justifying delays in the operations in question.[284] However, one might wonder whether, in the light of the case law just discussed, other 'wholly exceptional circumstances' might be invoked to render the interpretation of the promptness requirement established by Article 5(3) ECHR more flexible. Maritime SAR operations of a large number of people or under particularly adverse conditions of navigation would be another example of 'exceptional circumstances'. Moreover, in interpreting the pertinent provisions of the Convention, the Court has shown to attribute a certain relevance to the specific conditions which may present themselves at sea on each occasion.[285]

One remaining aspect of the right to liberty and security which may be problematic in the context of counter-smuggling and counter-trafficking operations is the right of any arrested person to be "informed promptly, in a language that he understands, of the reasons of his arrest and of any charges against him" set forth by Article 5(2) ECHR. According to the ECtHR's well-established case law, this provision contains the elementary safeguard that any person arrested should know why he is being deprived of his liberty, implying that any person arrested must be told the essential legal and factual grounds for his arrest, so as to be able to apply to a court to challenge its lawfulness.[286] However, while this information must be conveyed 'promptly', it need not to be related in its entirety by the arresting officer at the very moment of the arrest. Whether the content and promptness of the information conveyed were sufficient is to be assessed in each case according to its special features.[287]

There is no question about the fact that smugglers and traffickers must be informed in a language that they understand, but it is not clear when the information must be given to them. In *Medvedyev*, the Court accepted that it might take 13 days before a person arrested on the high seas could be presented before a judge or another qualified officer. The judgment did not address any issue under Article 5(2) ECHR; however, as regards these essential obligations, the Court could hardly endorse the extensive interpretation adopted in the *Medvedyev* case in relation to the obligations under Article 5(3) ECHR. Thus,

---

284 See in this regard Papastavridis, "EUNAVFOR MED Operation Sophia," 153.

285 See again Treves, "Human Rights," 8. Regarding the scarce inclination of many judges of the ECtHR to consider the specific needs of maritime interdiction operations for the purposes of a more flexible application of the Convention see, however, Douglas Guilfoyle, "ECHR Rights at Sea: *Medvedyev and Others v. France*," *EJIL: Talk!*, April 19, 2010.

286 Cf., e.g., ECtHR, *Ladent v Poland*, Appl. No. 11036/03, judgment of March 18, 2008, para. 63.

287 See again ECtHR, *Ladent*, para. 63 and, *mutatis mutandis*, ECtHR, *Murray v The United Kingdom*, Appl. No. 14310/88, judgment of October 28, 1994, para. 72 and *Čonka v Belgium*, Appl. No. 51564/99, judgment of February 5, 2002, para. 50.

the naval forces that make such apprehensions on the high seas should embark specialized translators to perform this function because failure to provide intelligible information under Article 5(2) may have long-term effects on the fairness of any subsequent trial.[288]

6 *The Right to a Fair Trial*

Once they have been brought before the judiciary, alleged smugglers and traffickers enjoy the right to a 'fair trial' enshrined in Article 6 ECHR. The case law on this provision is very extensive, but there are two issues that may pose a particular problem in these cases: the access to legal assistance while in custody and the collection and admissibility at trial of criminal evidence.

6.1 The Access to Legal Assistance

In the landmark judgment *Salduz v Turkey*, the ECtHR found a violation of Article 6 ECHR on account of the lack of legal assistance to the applicant while in police custody.[289] The Court considered that even where compelling reasons might exceptionally justify the denial of access to a lawyer, such a restriction, whatever its justification, must not have unduly prejudiced the rights of the accused. The rationale behind the *Salduz* judgment is that the rights of defense would in principle be irretrievably prejudiced when incriminating statements made during a police interview without access to a lawyer were used as a basis for a conviction.

After *Medvedyev*, where the Court did not apply very strict scrutiny under Article 5 on account of the 'exceptional circumstances' of an arrest on the high seas, we can assume that the same would be true in the context of Article 6. If exceptional circumstances may justify delays in bringing the detainee before a judge or another officer authorized to exercise judicial powers, it makes sense that the same reasoning be applied to legal assistance. However, the issue should be raised as to the lawfulness of any statement made by smugglers and traffickers while detained on board a ship without any form of legal assistance, even by radio or telephone. This question opens a wider discussion on the collection and admissibility at trial of criminal evidence, which could be particularly problematic when the initial phases of a criminal investigation are conducted on the high seas by military personnel.

288 See e.g. ECtHR, GC, *Pélissier and Sassi v France*, Appl. No. 25444/94, judgment of March 25, 1999, para. 51 and *Kamasinski v Austria*, Appl. No. 9783/82, judgment of December 19, 1989, paras. 72–77; for similar considerations in the context of counter-piracy operations conducted in the Indian Ocean by EU navies see Piedimonte Bodini, "Fighting," 839–840.

289 ECtHR, GC, *Salduz v Turkey*, Appl. No. 36391/02, judgment of November 27, 2008.

6.2 The Collection and Admissibility of Criminal Evidence

The question of the admissibility of evidence and its role in the fairness of criminal trials is not a new one. The relevant case law has been clearly summarized in the case *Gäfgen v Germany*.[290] The German courts refused to admit the confession obtained under duress but did not bar the use of the 'real evidence' obtained following the extorted confession. The Court therefore had to determine whether the use of the real evidence at trial had breached Mr. Gäfgen's rights under Article 6 ECHR.

The Grand Chamber recalled that, under Article 6, the Court should not examine the admissibility of evidence as such, which is left to the domestic courts, but only examine its impact on the overall fairness of the proceedings. It then confirmed that confessions obtained by methods in breach of Article 3, like the threat of torture, could never be admitted at trial because they rendered the proceedings as a whole unfair, irrespective of whether or not they were the only element relied upon.

On the other hand, as far as 'real evidence' is concerned, the test is somehow less strict. In *Gäfgen*, however, it was the applicant's new confession at the trial—after having been informed that all his earlier statements could not be used as evidence against him—which formed the basis for his conviction. The 'real evidence' in dispute had not been necessary to prove him guilty or determine his sentence. The proceedings as a whole had therefore not been unfair.

The sensitive issue of the collection of evidence, whether oral or 'real', must therefore be monitored with special care in the context of counter-trafficking and counter-smuggling operations. Such operations, in fact, are mainly carried out by military or by law enforcement units and not by experienced criminal investigators, and they may be more concerned with the tactical success of their operations than with their long-term judicial effects.[291]

7 *The Rights of Third Parties*

The fight against smuggling and trafficking raises many other questions under several Convention provisions. Indeed, in these cases, smugglers and traffickers are not the only stakeholders: third parties' rights are also involved, such as the right to privacy of private vessels legally sailing the Mediterranean and the right to property of ship owners used by illegal organizations, who equally have their rights recognized under the Convention.

---

290 ECtHR, GC, *Gäfgen v Germany*, Appl. No. 22978/05, judgment of June 1, 2010.

291 For similar considerations in the context of counter-piracy operations see again Piedimonte Bodini, "Fighting," 840–841.

7.1 The Right to Privacy

As regards the right to privacy, before intercepting suspected vessels, the military and law enforcement agents usually put them under surveillance: thus, all sorts of craft are subject to monitoring of radio and phone communications, including those exchanged within Libyan territory, which are intercepted on regular basis. Assuming that State jurisdiction can be established, all these actions might fall within the scope of Article 8 ECHR, which protects the right to respect for private life.

The interception of people's conversations and secret video surveillance are both considered by the ECtHR to constitute an interference with the right to privacy.[292] According to the ECtHR's well-established case law, such an interference breaches Article 8 unless it is "in accordance with the law", pursues one or more of the legitimate aims referred to in Article 8(2)[293] and it is "necessary in a democratic society" to achieve those aims.

Surveillance of suspect pirates seems to find its legal basis in customary international law,[294] but it is not clear if the same is also true for surveillance of smugglers and traffickers or if a legal basis can be found in UN Security Council Resolution No. 2240 (2015).

As to the question whether an interference is "necessary in a democratic society" in pursuit of a legitimate aim, the ECtHR considers that powers to conduct secret surveillance are tolerated under Article 8 only to the extent that they are subject to adequate and effective guarantees against abuse, the assessment of which depends on all the circumstances of the case, such as the nature, scope, and duration of the measures; the grounds required for ordering them; the authorities competent to authorize, carry out, and supervise them; and the kind of remedy provided by national law.[295]

In the context of the ECHR it seems to be safe to assume that the fight against maritime smuggling and trafficking would be considered by the Court as a legitimate aim and that the forms of surveillance mentioned above would be considered necessary when monitoring maritime zones plagued by illicit activities. However, there could be a problem when it comes to the procedures for supervising those surveillance measures as well as questions concerning their duration and scope.

---

292 See, e.g., ECtHR, *Khan v The United Kingdom*, Appl. No. 35394/97, judgment of May 12, 2000, paras. 26–28.

293 Cf. Article 8(2) ECHR.

294 Cf. again Piedimonte Bodini, "Fighting," 835.

295 See, for instance, ECtHR, *Klass et al. v Germany*, Appl. No. 5029/71, judgment of September 6, 1978, paras. 49–50 and *Weber and Saravia v Germany*, Appl. No. 54934/00, judgment of June 29, 2006, para. 106.

The Court considers the interception of communications to be an area where abuse is potentially easy. It therefore requires that it be subject, in principle, to the supervision of a judge or, exceptionally, of another authority that must be independent from the executive power and provided with "sufficient powers and competence to exercise effective and continuous control."[296]

Thus, the interception of smugglers and traffickers communications must be duly authorized and supervised by a judge or some other independent authority. Furthermore, it seems that a judge could authorize Navy commanders to intercept telephone communications in the areas under their responsibility only within a specific time frame and only where *prima facie* criminal evidence can be found.[297]

In recent investigations conducted by Italian public prosecutors in Palermo who successfully detected a criminal network which smuggled migrants from Libya, Eritrea, Ethiopia, Sudan and Israel to Sicily[298] and from there towards northern Italy and eventually to northern Europe,[299] evidence on the crime of smuggling was gathered through wiretapping.[300] The Italian Supreme Court of Cassation has admitted evidence obtained through wiretapping where the calls were made either from Italian telephones or to Italian telephones. This activity is not in breach of the national sovereignty of third countries, as the wiretapping took place wholly on Italian territory,[301] and it effectively complies with the principle of territoriality of jurisdiction and with Article 4 of Council Framework Decision No. 2002/946/JHA, which states that EU Member States have jurisdiction over the crime of smuggling, *inter alia*, if part of the criminal activity is committed on their territory.[302]

296 For instance, a mixed parliamentary commission of the *Bundestag* (see again ECtHR, *Klass*, para. 56) and the British Interception of Communications Commissioner did pass the Court's test (ECtHR, *Kennedy v The United Kingdom*, Appl. No. 26839/05, judgment of May 18, 2010, para. 169), while public prosecutors in Romania did not (see, for instance, ECtHR, *Dumitru Popescu v Romania (No. 2)*, Appl. No. 71525/01, judgment of April 26, 2007, para. 71 and *Vasilescu v Romania*, Appl. No. 27053/95, judgment of May 22, 1998, paras. 40–41).

297 See again Piedimonte Bodini, "Fighting," 836.

298 See Tribunal of Palermo, Direzione Distrettuale Antimafia, Public Prosecutor Decree of arrest under Article 384 Italian Criminal Code, May 30, 2016, 16.

299 Ivi, 2.

300 Ivi, 20.

301 Ivi, 20–21. See also Supreme Court of Cassation, Section IV, judgment No. 32924, July 29, 2004 and Supreme Court of Cassation, Section V, judgment No. 4401, October 21, 1998.

302 Cf. Article 4(1) Council Framework Decision No. 2002/946/JHA, November 28, 2002, on the strengthening of the penal framework to prevent the facilitation of unauthorised entry, transit and residence 2002 *OJEU* L 328/1. On jurisdictional issues more will be said below, Part III, para. 1.

7.2 The Right to Private Property

In the context of naval operations in the Mediterranean, it seems that the destruction of boats has been considered a relevant tool for suppressing and deterring the smuggling of migrants and the trafficking of human beings.[303] As said above, in order to achieve the goal of disrupting the business model of migrant smugglers and human traffickers, Operation *Sophia* military vessels were endowed with the powers to board, search, seize and divert vessels suspected of being used for migrant smuggling and human trafficking while also being allowed to render them inoperable.[304] A question arises as to whether the destruction of boats is an appropriate criminal law measure in compliance with international human rights law.

Destruction of boats during or after the interception may prove problematic as demonstrated by concerns already raised in relation to the consistency of counter-piracy operations with the right to property.[305] In the absence of a legal basis, in fact, it may entail violations of the right to property enshrined in Article 1 Protocol 1 ECHR. While the UNCLOS provides a legal basis for the seizure of pirate ships,[306] it does not do so in relation to ships suspected of being used for migrant smuggling and human trafficking. Even if all the boats used by smugglers and traffickers should happen to be unregistered ships, the UNCLOS only envisages the right to visit (i.e. stop, board, and search) such ships;[307] it does not accord States the power to seize or destroy them. Furthermore, as said above, Article 8(7) Smuggling Protocol reiterates the general discipline coded in the UNCLOS and does not justify disposal of the ship.[308] Moreover, the destruction of the *corpus delicti* in the absence of criminal conviction is not compatible with the cardinal criminal law principle of presumption of innocence.[309]

Gaps in the international law of the sea as to the right to seize and dispose of smugglers and traffickers' vessels are only partially filled by Security Council Resolution No. 2240 (2015), which accords States the right to inspect, seize and eventually dispose of vessels suspected of being used for migrant smuggling

303 Cf. S/RES/2240 (2015), para. 8 and Council Decision No. 2015/778/CFSP, Article 1(1) and 2(2)(c).
304 Cf. Council Decision No. 2015/778/CFSP, Articles 2(2)(b)(i) and (ii).
305 See again Piedimonte Bodini, "Fighting," 842.
306 Cf. Article 105 UNCLOS.
307 Cf. Article 110 (1)(d) UNCLOS.
308 See above, Introduction. For a different opinion see Marta Bo, "Repressing Migrant Smuggling by the UN Security Council and EU Naval Military Operation *Sophia*: Some Reflections on Jurisdiction and Human Rights," *EJIL: Talk!*, November 3, 2017, 2.
309 Ibid., 2.

and human trafficking on the high seas off the coast of Libya.[310] However, Decision No. 2015/778 does not reproduce such authorization: while on the high seas vessels taking part in Operation *Sophia* have the power to board, search, seize and divert,[311] the power of disposal would be allowed only if Operation *Sophia* had moved into the territorial and/or internal waters (Phase 2B) and territory of Libya (Phase 3).[312] However, Operation *Sophia* never saw a transition to Phases 2B and 3 because of the position of Russia and China, which possessed veto power in the UN Security Council: its vessels only carried out their activities on the high seas off the coast of Libya.

It remains to be determined what measures can be adopted *vis-à-vis* ships flying a foreign flag if, following an inspection, the suspicions prove to be well founded. Resolution No. 2240 (2015) expressly authorizes only the seizure of the boat, but specifies that other measures, including the disposal of the ship, should be taken "in accordance with applicable international law with due consideration of the interests of any third parties who have acted in good faith."[313] This provision proves to be particularly obscure.[314] On the one hand, it could be assumed that coercive activities other than seizure are not covered by the authorization, and can therefore be implemented only within the limits of what is allowed by the rules of general international law or by relevant international treaties (and therefore only with prior authorization of the flag State). On the other hand, it could be assumed that the authorization of the Security Council also extends to coercive measures other than seizure, provided that they are adopted in compliance with any other relevant international rules, such as those concerning the protection of human rights and the prohibition of *refoulement*.

The second and more extensive interpretation was eventually preferred. The Italian Commander of Operation *Sophia*, Mr. Credendino, stated, in fact, that vessels used by the traffickers and smugglers are systematically destroyed by the assets allocated to Operation *Sophia* once the rescue of migrants has concluded, without any distinction depending on whether they are unregistered vessels or vessels flying a foreign flag.[315] However, this *modus operandi* does not seem entirely consistent with Resolution No. 2240 (2015).

---

310 Cf. the Security Council Resolution No. 2240 (2015), paras. 7–8. For a different opinion, see again Bo, "Repressing," 2.

311 Article 2(2)(b).

312 Article 2(2)(c).

313 Cf. Resolution No. 2240 (2015), para 8.

314 Gestri, "EUNAVFOR MED," 41–42.

315 Cf. Hearing of the Admiral of Division Enrico Credendino, Commander of the mission EUNAVFOR MED—Operation *Sophia*, Parliamentary commission of inquiry on the

As said, the destruction of vessels used by traffickers and smugglers can raise some problems as regards Article 1 Protocol No. 1 ECHR.[316] It seems difficult to argue that a systematic destruction of vessels used for these illicit activities without any further assessment as regards the rights of third parties acting in good faith can meet the necessity and proportionality requirements imposed for each restriction of property.[317] Thus, for instance, there could be problems where a ship used by smugglers or traffickers but belonging to someone else were not returned to the legitimate *bona fide* owner after having been seized by a State's authorities[318] or in the event of an acquittal of the alleged smuggler or trafficker. The ECtHR established a clear principle in this respect in the *Tendam v Spain* case.[319] A man indicted on several criminal charges and later acquitted was denied compensation by Spanish judicial authorities for property seized during the criminal proceedings and returned in poor condition. The Court found that the judicial authorities were responsible for the property seized and had a duty to inventory it and maintain it with good care. Moreover, it held that the burden of proof regarding missing or damaged property lies with those authorities.[320]

Part III. The Exercise of Criminal Jurisdiction over Migrant Smugglers and Human Traffickers

1 *The Jurisdiction over Transnational Crimes on the High Seas: General Issues*

Counter-smuggling and counter-trafficking operations in the Mediterranean should also aim to apprehend and try smugglers and traffickers before a domestic court. Due to the fact that the Libyan judicial system is not currently able to perform its functions because of the civil war,[321] other venues for the trial of suspected smugglers and traffickers must be found.

---

system of reception, identification, expulsion and on the conditions of detention of migrants and on the use of public resources, Meeting No. 82 of April 6, 2017, 9.

316 On this issue see also Butler and Ratcovich, "Operation Sophia," 253–254.

317 The relevant test adopted by the Court in the context of Article 1 Protocol No. 1 ECHR is the following: (i) whether there has been an interference with property rights; (ii) whether the interference has a legal basis; (iii) whether it is in the general interest; and (iv) whether it is proportionate, i.e., whether a fair balance has been struck between the individual right and the general interest.

318 See, *mutatis mutandis*, ECtHR, *Bowler International Unit v France*, Appl. No. 1946/06, judgment of July 23, 2009, para. 46.

319 ECtHR, *Tendam v Spain*, Appl. No. 25720/05, judgment of July 13, 2010, para. 53.

320 Ivi, paras. 53–57.

321 See above, Introduction.

In the *Lotus* case of 1927, the Permanent Court of International Justice (PCIJ) maintained that international law allows States to extend the jurisdiction of their civil courts to persons, property and acts outside their territory, leaving them a wide measure of discretion. Following the reasoning of the Court, States' discretion is only limited whether prohibitive rules can be found in the specific case.[322] The Court, however, did not consider the same principle such as applicable to criminal jurisdiction, which has always been considered an essential feature of a State's territorial sovereignty.[323] Thus, in the case of crimes perpetrated on a ship on the high seas, the freedom given to States to define the scope of domestic criminal jurisdiction[324] must be reconciled with the flag State's interest in prosecution. In the absence of a significant connection with the crime, extraterritorial exercise of jurisdiction would constitute an abuse of right.[325]

There are cases in which international law itself authorizes the exercise of universal criminal jurisdiction to facilitate the punishment of crimes that endanger interests of the international community as a whole, such as in the case of piracy *juris gentium*, which has always been considered a threat to mankind.[326] However, international law does not recognize the exercise of universal criminal jurisdiction in the case of transnational crimes such as migrant smuggling and human trafficking.[327] Thus, the exercise of extraterritorial

322 PCIJ, *SS Lotus* (*France v Turkey*), judgment of September 7, 1927, 18–19.

323 Ibid., 20.

324 The existence of such a regime is acknowledged, among others, by Chiara Amalfitano, *Conflitti di giurisdizione e riconoscimento delle decisioni penali nell'Unione europea* (Milan: Giuffrè, 2006), 1. *Contra* see Rüdiger Wolfrum, "The Decentralized Prosecution of International Offences Through National Courts," in *War Crimes in International Law*, eds. Yoram Dinstein and Mala Tabory (The Hague: Nijhoff, 1996), 233, according to whom the international prohibition of interference in the internal affairs of other States prevents domestic courts from judging crimes having no connection whatsoever with the forum State.

325 Cf., among others, Iain Cameron, *The Protective Principle of International Criminal Jurisdiction* (Aldershot: Dartmouth, 1994), 337. Other authors maintain that the exercise of extraterritorial criminal jurisdiction is subject to a 'reasonableness' test: cf. Cedric Ryngaert, *Jurisdiction in International Law* (2nd edn. Oxford: OUP, 2015), 29. On the issue see again Annoni, "International," 183–184.

326 Cf. ICJ, *Arrest Warrant of 11 April 2000* (*Democratic Republic of the Congo v Belgium*), judgment of February 14, 2002, *ICJ Reports*, 2002, Separate Opinion of Judge Guillaume, 37 and Declaration of Judge Ranjeva, 56.

327 See again above, Introduction. Cf. also, as regards migrants smuggling, Meijers Committee, "Military action against human smugglers: legal questions concerning the EUNAVFOR Med operation," September 23, 2015, www.statewatch.org/news/2015/sep/eu-meijers-cttee-eunavfor.pdf (last accessed April 19, 2019). With respect to human trafficking, see ECtHR, *J. et al. v Austria*, Appl. No. 58216/12, judgment of January 17, 2017, para. 114.

criminal jurisdiction with respect to these crimes committed on the high seas on foreign-flagged vessels requires an effective link between the criminal offence and the State willing to exercise its criminal jurisdiction. This can be seen in the case of States of destination of vessels engaged in migrant smuggling and human trafficking across the Mediterranean, that is, EU Member States. The same holds true in the case of unregistered or unflagged vessels (such as inflatable boats, rafts and dinghies), which are often used in order to smuggle migrants to the EU. In order to lawfully arrest and subject the offenders to their criminal jurisdiction, the States concerned must have enacted legislation in accordance with a well-accepted principle of international jurisdiction that criminalizes migrant smuggling and human trafficking, even on unflagged vessels on the high seas.[328]

It remains to be clarified to what extent States are actually required to exercise criminal jurisdiction over smugglers of migrants and traffickers of human beings under international law, as opposed to merely being permitted to do so. Such an obligation may stem, first of all, from international human rights law: customary and treaty rules require States not only to respect, but also to ensure respect of human rights by other States and non-State actors.[329] States have an obligation to do everything in their power to prevent, investigate and repress violations of human rights perpetrated within their jurisdiction. It is a due diligence obligation whose respect is commensurate to the concrete possibilities for the State to obtain the result required by the international obligation.

The obligation to repress violations of the human rights of migrants is binding first of all on the State of origin of the smuggling and trafficking, insofar as regards acts perpetrated in its territorial or internal waters. Given the condition of the local judicial system, however, Libya could not reasonably be expected to take charge of prosecuting all crimes committed within its jurisdiction. Libyan authorities fulfil their due diligence obligation when they permit foreign States

328 In this respect, among others, cf. Papastavridis, "EUNAVFOR Operation Sophia and the International Law," 68–69; Churchill and Lowe, *The Law of the Sea*, 214; Yoshifumi Tanaka, *The International Law of the Sea* (Cambridge: CUP, 2012), 162. *Contra* see the US current practice: United States Department of the Navy, "The Commander's Handbook on the Law of Naval Operations," Doc. NWP 1-14M, July 2007, para. 3.11.2.3; and, in the legal literature, among others, Andrea De Guttry, *Lo status della nave da Guerra in tempo di pace* (Milan: Giuffrè, 1994), 183.

329 Human Rights Commission, "Basic Principles and Guidelines on the Right to a Remedy and Reparations for Victims of Violations of International Human Rights and Humanitarian Law," January 18, 2000, UN Doc. E/CN.4/2000/62, Annex, Article 1. This provision builds on those included in major human rights treaties (e.g. CCPR, Article 2; ECHR, Article 1; and American Convention on Human Rights (ACHR), Article 1).

to capture and punish smugglers of migrants using vessels flying the flag of that State.

In principle, EU States taking part in operations against the smuggling and trafficking of migrants across the Mediterranean have the authority—but not also a specific obligation—to repress human rights violations committed outside their jurisdiction. However, the obligation to exercise criminal jurisdiction over smugglers and traffickers apprehended on the high seas may also stem from international criminal law conventions or EU instruments. Examples of such instruments are Directive No. 2002/90/EC, defining the facilitation of unauthorized entry, transit and residence[330] and Council Framework Decision No. 2002/946/JHA, on the strengthening of the penal framework to prevent the facilitation of unauthorized entry, transit and residence.[331] Thus, for instance, Article 4 Framework Decision No. 2002/946/JHA provides that "each Member State shall take the measures necessary to establish its jurisdiction with regard to the infringements (…) committed (a) in whole or in part within its territory; (b) by one of its nationals, or (c) for the benefit of a legal person established in the territory of that Member State."

Furthermore, criminal conducts perpetrated on the high seas off the coast of Libya may trigger the application of the UNTOC, which binds States parties to criminalize participation in an organized group whose purpose is to commit "serious transnational crimes."[332] According to Article 15 UNTOC, States parties must establish jurisdiction over such crimes when they are committed in their territory or on board a vessel flying their flag.[333] The Convention also contains the *aut dedere aut judicare* clause but in this case the duty to prosecute only arises if the State party does not extradite the alleged offender "solely on the ground that he or she is one of its nationals."[334] The provision refers to the territory of States parties but the rule is also applicable with respect to military vessels of those States. Accordingly, States parties to the UNTOC have a specific obligation to repress those crimes—even if the alleged smuggler is apprehended on the high seas—when the alleged offender is found on the territory of the State of his nationality and extradition is refused because of his nationality. The obligation seems to be of relevance because the UNTOC has been ratified by all EU Member States and by all Mediterranean States (Libya included), but it is strictly limited to citizens of that State. This does not

330 Council Directive No. 2002/90/EC, November 28, 2002, defining the facilitation of unauthorized entry, transit and residence, *OJEU* L 328/17.

331 See again Council Framework Decision No. 2002/946/JHA.

332 Articles 2(b), 3(2) and 5 UNTOC.

333 Article 15(1)(a) and 15(1)(b) UNTOC.

334 Article 15(3) and Article 16(10) UNTOC.

mean, however, that States parties to the UNTOC have to prosecute every single smuggler or trafficker they apprehend: the due diligence obligation to repress human rights violations may well be fulfilled by handing the suspect over to another State willing to exercise criminal jurisdiction.

Finally, migrant smuggling and human trafficking may also come within the scope of application of the 1988 Convention for the Suppression of Unlawful Acts against the Safety of Maritime Navigation.[335] Although this latter instrument was drafted in order to combat international terrorism,[336] the punishment of the offences described in Article 3 of the Convention (which include performing acts of violence against persons on board a ship, thus endangering the safety of navigation) was not made conditional on the existence of a specific terrorist intent. Under Article 6 of the Convention, the State in which an alleged offender is present is obligated to submit the case to its competent authorities for the purpose of prosecution or to extradite the person in question to another State that has jurisdiction.[337] This *aut dedere aut judicare* rule also applies to situations in which the crime is not in any way linked to the State in which the perpetrator is currently present.[338] Although the provision explicitly refers to the 'territory' of States parties, it is likely that the rule will also apply when the alleged offender is on board a military vessel belonging to a State party.[339] Consequently, whenever a State party to the Convention captures a smuggler or a trafficker it will be obliged to prosecute them unless it transfers them to another State willing to exercise criminal jurisdiction.

The aforementioned international treaties have been widely ratified by States participating in the EU naval missions on the high seas off the coast of Libya. However, despite this, to date suspected smugglers and traffickers apprehended in the context of operations *Themis* and *Sophia* have been

335 Convention for the Suppression of Unlawful Acts against the Safety of Maritime Navigation, Rome, March 10, 1988, entered into force on March 1, 1992, *UNTS* vol. 1678, 201. Cf. Tullio Treves, "The Rome Convention for the Suppression of Unlawful Acts against the Safety of Maritime Navigation," in *Maritime Terrorism and International Law*, ed. Natalino Ronzitti (Dordrecht: Nijhoff, 1990), 69 and Francesco Francioni, "Maritime Terrorism and International Law: The Rome Convention of 1988," *German Yearbook of International Law* 31 (1988): 263.

336 Natalino Ronzitti, "The *Enrica Lexie* Incident: Law of the Sea and Immunity of State Officials Issues," *Italian Yearbook of International Law* 22 (2012): 9.

337 Article 10 of the Convention.

338 Articles 6(4) of the Convention. On the *aut dedere aut judicare* obligation see Andrea Caligiuri, *L'obbligo* aut dedere aut judicare *nel diritto internazionale* (Milan: Giuffrè, 2012).

339 *Contra* Saiful Karim, "Is There an International Obligation to Prosecute Pirates?," *Netherlands International Law Review* 58 (2011): 399.

prosecuted just before Italian criminal courts. After having been caught by multinational missions, in fact, they were all transferred to the Italian authorities to be prosecuted.[340]

This practice is brought about by a number of factors. Firstly, the domestic law of many States is not consistent with their international obligations, as they lack either legislation criminalizing migrant smuggling and human trafficking or appropriate heads of jurisdiction for judging offences committed on the high seas off the coast of Libya.[341] In legal orders where the obligations to make certain conducts punishable and to establish jurisdiction over a given crime are not self-executing, this constitutes a serious obstacle to prosecution. Secondly, it is worth considering that, even when a crime falls within the scope of their mandatory jurisdiction according to international criminal law treaties, States Parties are not obliged to bring the case before their courts unless the alleged perpetrator is present on their territory (or military vessel), and nothing compels them to accept the transfer of a suspect detained by another State.[342]

2 *The Prosecution of Suspected Smugglers and Traffickers Apprehended on the High Seas*

As said above,[343] neither UN Security Council Resolution No. 2240 (2015) nor European Council Decision No. 2015/778 expressly permits the exercise of adjudicatory jurisdiction against suspected smugglers and traffickers apprehended in the context of the operations carried out in the Central Mediterranean.[344] That being the legal framework established at the UN and EU level, in practice a number of individuals suspected of migrant smuggling and human trafficking have been apprehended by ships participating in EU operations and handed over to the Italian authorities.

340 EU External Action Service, https://www.operationsophia.eu/ (last accessed April 19, 2019).

341 Cf. Security Council Resolution No. 1918 (2010). Several States subsequently changed their law to allow domestic courts to judge Somali pirates (cf. UN Doc. S/2012/177, March 26, 2012). See also Giovanni Cocco, "Dal pirata *hostis humani generis* alla pirateria contemporanea. Verso un diritto penale universale?," *Rivista italiana di diritto e procedura penale* 2 (2012): 409.

342 For similar considerations as regards EU counter-piracy operations see Annoni, "International," 183.

343 See above, Part II, para. 5.

344 On the issue cf. among others, Matilde Ventrella, "The Impact of Operation Sophia on the Exercise of Criminal Jurisdiction against Migrant Smugglers and Human Traffickers," in *Questions of International Law, Zoom-in* 30 (2016): 10 and Gestri, "EUNAVFOR MED," 47–48.

From a legal perspective, however, this practice gives rise to the issue of whether an appropriate legal basis for asserting criminal jurisdiction over these individuals exists under Italian law: it is not always clear, in fact, on which basis Italian adjudicatory jurisdiction is established with respect to acts of smuggling and trafficking entirely performed on the high seas.

The extent of State criminal jurisdiction over transnational crimes committed at sea essentially depends on domestic law, which may constitute the implementation of precise international obligations, but it may also be the result of independent determinations by the national legislator. Thus, the legislator may well decide to extend the jurisdiction of its own criminal courts to events that have taken place on board ships flying a third State flag. The principle of exclusive jurisdiction of the flag state on the high seas, codified in Article 92 UNCLOS, only refers, in fact, to the enforcement jurisdiction and implies exclusively a prohibition against adopting coercive measures with respect to the ship; it does not preclude the possibility for any foreign State to exercise its own adjudicatory jurisdiction and to investigate (on its territory) the crimes committed on board during navigation on the high seas.[345]

The Italian criminal system is based upon the general principle of the territoriality of criminal law (Article 6 of the Criminal Code). For the purposes of criminal law enforcement, ships flying the Italian flag on the high seas are considered as Italian territory.[346] Moreover, the majority of legal scholars also include the territorial sea[347] and internal waters in the notion of 'territory of the State' under Article 6 Italian Criminal Code.[348] It is not clear, however, whether crimes of aiding illegal immigration[349] and trafficking in human beings[350] committed in the contiguous zone fall within Italian jurisdiction, considering that, according to the letter of Article 33 UNCLOS, in that sea area the State should exercise police powers only insofar as they are necessary to prevent and repress crimes committed on its territory or in its territorial sea.[351]

345 Cf., among others, Laura Magi, "Criminal Conduct on the High Seas: Is a General Rule on Jurisdiction to Prosecute still Missing?," *Rivista di diritto internazionale* 98 (2015): 82; Enrico Zamuner, *La tutela delle navi private nel diritto internazionale* (Naples: Scientifica, 2015), 152. *Contra*: Ronzitti, "The *Enrica Lexie*," 14.

346 See Article 4(2) Italian Criminal Code.

347 Cf., *ex plurimis*, Fabio Dean, *Norma penale e territorio. Gli elementi di territorialità in relazione alla struttura del reato* (Milano: Giuffrè, 1963), 200.

348 Cf. Gestri, "EUNAVFOR MED," 49.

349 Cf. Article 12 Legislative Decree No. 286/1998.

350 Cf. Article 601 Italian Criminal Code.

351 On this issue cf. Laura Salvadego, "Controllo marittimo dell'immigrazione clandestina e giurisdizione penale del giudice italiano," *Rivista di diritto internazionale* 93 (2010): 1154 and Jasmine Coppens, "Interception of Migrant Boats at Sea," in *'Boat Refugees' and*

The exercise of national criminal jurisdiction over crimes committed by a foreigner abroad (or on a vessel flying the flag of a third State on the high seas) has an exceptional character. Under Article 10 Italian Criminal Code, a foreigner who commits a crime against a foreigner outside the Italian territory can be prosecuted in Italy only when several conditions are met: (a) the alleged offender must be in Italy; (b) the offence must be one for which a minimum sentence of three years of imprisonment is established; (c) there must be a request from the Minister of Justice (or the complaint of the victim of the offence if required under Italian law).

Apart from these situations, in accordance with Article 7 Italian Criminal Code, foreigners can be prosecuted before Italian courts with regard to a set of specific offences affecting essential national interests (included in Article 7(1–4)), or with respect to "any other offence for which special provisions of law or international conventions provide for the applicability of Italian law" (Article 7(5) Italian Criminal Code).

Article 7 Italian Criminal Code has thus been invoked in order to justify an extension of Italian jurisdiction. Absent any relevant provision in the UNCLOS, according to some scholars, the assertion of Italian criminal jurisdiction in respect of persons on board flagless ships on the high sea could be justified under Article 7(5) Italian Criminal Code if read in conjunction with Article 8(7) Smuggling Protocol.[352] On the other hand, the Court of Cassation has sometimes extended Italian jurisdiction in cases involving the crime of participation in an organized criminal association (Article 416 Italian Criminal Code) on the basis of the joint application of Article 7(5) Italian Criminal Code and Article 15(2)(c) UNTOC.[353]

Article 15 UNTOC provides for some instances of compulsory jurisdiction already envisaged by Italian legislation,[354] and it also allows the State to extend its criminal jurisdiction to offenses of criminal association committed abroad but aimed at the commission of serious crimes in the territory of the State.[355]

Migrants at Sea: A Comprehensive Approach. Integrating Maritime Security with Human Rights, eds. Violeta Moreno-Lax and Efthymios Papastavridis (Leiden: Nijhoff, 2017), 206.

352 See, in this respect, Umberto Leanza and Francesca Graziani, "Poteri di *enforcement* e di *jurisdiction* in materia di traffico di migranti via mare: aspetti operativi nell'attività di contrasto," *La Comunità internazionale* 69 (2014): 191.

353 See Italian Court of Cassation, Criminal Section I, judgment of February 28, 2014, No. 14510, *Rivista di diritto internazionale* (2014): 939.

354 Article 15(1) UNTOC provides for an obligation to prosecute in the case of events occurring on the territory of the State or on board a ship flying the flag of the State, or an aircraft registered under the laws of the State.

355 Under Article 15(2)(c) UNTOC a State party may establish its jurisdiction when the offence is one of those established in accordance with Article 5(1) UNTOC and is committed outside its territory with a view to the commission of a serious crime within its territory.

This is a particularly relevant hypothesis in the case we are dealing with, considering that journeys to cross the Mediterranean are usually organized and managed by criminal networks in order to favor the illegal entry of migrants into Italy or their exploitation in that State. However, in order to become fully operative in the Italian legal system, international norms empowering the State to exercise its jurisdiction require the adoption of specific national legislation which would extend the scope of application of Italian criminal law to the cases envisaged as being merely 'optional' under international law.[356] However, Italian Law No. 146 of March 16, 2006, implementing the UNTOC and its Protocols in the Italian legal order, does not contain any such provision.[357] Furthermore, it does not seem that any other provision of international conventions can be relevant for this purpose.[358]

As far as ships without nationality are concerned, Italian case law does not seem to follow the theory according to which flagless ships *per se* can be subjected to the adjudicative jurisdiction of any State.[359] Accordingly, the assertion of Italian jurisdiction *vis-à-vis* suspected smugglers on board ships without nationality on the high seas should be founded on one of the grounds envisaged by the Italian Criminal Code.[360]

In this connection, it is worth highlighting a trend in Italian case law to interpret the territoriality principle broadly, so as to establish the Italian jurisdiction *vis-à-vis* foreigners apprehended on the high seas (both on foreign flagged vessels and on flagless vessels). This is made possible by the broad scope of application of Article 6(2) Italian Criminal Code, which provides that a crime is considered to have been committed in the territory of the State when the act or the omission constituting the crime was at least 'in part' perpetrated there, or the effects of the offense occurred there.[361]

---

356 On this issue see Alessandra Annoni, "Traffico di migranti via mare: l'ambito di applicazione della legge penale italiana," *Rivista di diritto della navigazione* 44 (2015): 420.

357 A legislative intervention to fill this gap would certainly be appropriate, also given the Security Council's recent call on the Member States "to consider establishing jurisdiction to end the impunity of [traffickers in human beings] in line with Article 15 of the UN Convention against Transnational Organized Crime": cf. Resolution No. 2388 (2017), November 21, 2017, para. 4.

358 An in-depth analysis in this respect is provided by Alessandra Annoni, "Il ruolo delle operazioni *Triton* e *Sophia* nella repressione della tratta di esseri umani e del traffico di migranti nel Mediterraneo centrale," *Diritto dell'Unione Europea* 4 (2017): 851–852.

359 Cf. Gestri, "EUNAVFOR MED," 33.

360 Ivi, 32–33 and 49. See above, Part III, para. 1.

361 See Marcello Mastrojeni, "I limiti spaziali di applicazione della legge penale e i rapporti con giurisdizioni straniere," in *La legge, penale, il reato, il reo, la persona offesa*, ed. Giancarlo De Vero (Turin: Giappichelli, 2010), 101.

Indeed, Italian courts have declared their jurisdiction when the smugglers or traffickers are part of a criminal network with some ramification in Italian territory and at least a fraction of the criminal conduct attributable to the network took place in Italian territory. Thus, for instance, jurisdiction would be exercised in the case of a mother ship operating in connection with smaller vessels departing from the Italian coast or territorial waters,[362] or, more frequently, vessels escorted by the mother ship which have penetrated into Italian waters,[363] and in the case of complicity in the crime of persons located in Italy,[364] whose communications with the smugglers on the high seas had for instance been intercepted.[365] In these situations, Italian jurisdiction is extended to all the participants in the crime, including the smugglers or traffickers operating on the high seas who never entered Italian territory.

Furthermore, according to well-established case law of the Supreme Court of Cassation, the jurisdiction of Italian courts over the crime of aiding illegal immigration cannot be challenged if part of the criminal acts have been committed in Italian territory, even indirectly, through the innocent intermediation of rescuers.[366] In this case, the landing of irregular migrants on Italian coasts represents the execution of the last part of a criminal plan organized by the smugglers and traffickers, who—by abandoning migrants on the high seas aboard crumbling vessels—are deemed to have created the conditions for their rescue and subsequent entry into Italy. As said above, in fact, the organization of rescue activities implies a specific obligation for the coastal State.[367] On the basis of complex legal reasoning, the conduct of the rescuers leading to the disembarkation of the migrants in Italy should be considered as the action of an *autore mediato*, i.e. a person used by smugglers in order to commit a crime, and who is not punishable for that crime. As a consequence, the illicit conduct is attributed exclusively to the smugglers operating on the high seas and the offense is regarded as partially committed in Italian territory.[368]

---

362 Court of Cassation, Criminal Section I, judgment of February 1, 2013, No. 16653, available at http://www.cortedicassazione.it (last accessed May 20, 2019).

363 Tribunal of Crotone, *Pamuk et al.*, judgment of September 27, 2001, *Rivista di diritto internazionale* (2001): 1155.

364 Court of Cassation, Criminal Section I, judgment of June 23, 2000, No. 4586 and Court of Cassation, Criminal Section I, judgment of August 20, 2014, No. 36052, both available at http://www.cortedicassazione.it (last accessed May 20, 2019).

365 On this issue see above, Part II, para. 7.1.

366 Court of Cassation, Criminal Section I, judgment of February 28, 2014, No. 14510, available at http://www.cortedicassazione.it (last accessed May 20, 2019).

367 On this issue see above, Part II, para. 8.

368 On this issue see Giuseppe Cataldi, "Giurisdizione e intervento in alto mare su navi impegnate nel traffico di migranti," *Giurisprudenza italiana* (2015): 1498 and Gestri, "EUNAVFOR MED," 50.

However, this interpretation, according to which the commander of a vessel engaged in EU operations at sea such as operations *Themis* and *Sophia* should likewise be regarded as an *autore mediato* when involved in SAR operations at sea, is not generally accepted by the legal literature.[369] The interpretation, in fact, does not seems to have a solid legal basis; rather, it was formulated for the sole purpose of somehow establishing Italian jurisdiction and preventing the impunity of smugglers and traffickers.

In the light of that uncertain legal picture, one must share the opinion of those who have advocated, for the sake of legal certainty, the introduction of *ad hoc* legislative rules governing the assertion of criminal jurisdiction over migrant smugglers or human traffickers apprehended on the high seas. This would be of relevance also in the context of Frontex missions and for Operation *Sophia*. Similar issues also came into play in the context of the EU counter-piracy Operation *Atalanta*. At the time, Italy decided to include a special provision in Article 5 of Decree Law No. 209 of December 30, 2008, on the extension of Italian participation in international missions; the provision in question, which is relevant for the purposes of Article 7(5) Criminal Code, makes the crimes of piracy and armed robbery at sea and offences connected to them punishable in Italy if such crimes are committed against the State or against Italian citizens or goods on the high seas or in territorial waters of other States in the areas where Operation *Atalanta* is conducted.[370] In fact, although a laudable effort has been undertaken by the National Anti-Mafia and Antiterrorist Division to clarify both the legal regime and the relevant Italian case law,[371] the guidelines provided are far from settling all these issues and they confirm the existence of areas in which the grounds for exercising criminal jurisdiction are questionable.[372]

3 *The Transfer of Suspects*

Although the seizing State has the primary right to try suspected smugglers and traffickers, it may transfer prisoners to another State willing to exercise its jurisdiction. In the framework of Operation *Sophia*, for instance, all decisions

369 See Annoni, "Il ruolo," 853–854.

370 See Annoni, "L'esercizio," 3.

371 Cf. National Prosecutor, "Proposte operative per la soluzione dei problemi di giurisdizione penale nazionale e possibilità di intervento," *Diritto penale contemporaneo*, January 9, 2014, as amended on July 16, 2015 and on October 28, 2015, with an introductory note by Filippo Spiezia, "Traffico di migranti via mare: le linee guida della Direzione nazionale antimafia per la soluzione dei problemi di giurisdizione penale e di intervento cautelare nei casi di attraversamento di acque internazionali," *Diritto penale contemporaneo* (2014).

372 Cf. Gestri, "EUNAVFOR MED," 51.

concerning the fate of suspects are taken by the EU Operation Commander.[373] Even in this case, however, a prisoner may be handed over to the authorities of a State other than the flag State of the seizing ship only if the latter State cannot, or does not wish to, prosecute the case.[374] As said above, in practice, all migrant smugglers and human traffickers apprehended in the context of EU naval operations are handed over to Italy.[375]

Although seizing States who are parties to one of the international conventions providing for the *aut dedere aut judicare* rule should swiftly open a preliminary investigation,[376] this obligation is rarely complied with. The decision to opt in favor of domestic prosecution is usually considered only once all attempts to have the suspect transferred to another State have failed.[377]

The decision as to the fate of prisoners should be taken quickly, as international human rights law, as noted, require all detained suspects to be brought promptly before a judge. As recognized by the ECtHR, however, when a suspect is arrested at sea, the particular circumstances of the arrest may allow a 'flexible' approach as regards the interpretation of the 'promptness' requirement as long as the delay is not unreasonable and it still guarantees the very essence of the rights of the detainee.[378] A transfer of suspected smugglers and traffickers may also take place as a result of an extradition request or of a European Arrest Warrant (EAW), if the crime has been committed in other EU Member States.[379] Article 1(1) EAW Framework Decision No. 2002/584/JHA defines the EAW as "a judicial decision issued by a Member State with a view to the arrest and surrender by another Member State of a requested person, for the purposes of conducting a criminal prosecution or executing a custodial

373 In the framework of NATO operations, by contrast, these decisions are taken by the seizing State without interference from the NATO chain of command: see, e.g., Matteo Tondini, "Stato di diritto e lotta alla pirateria nelle acque somale," *Diritto penale e processo* (2013): 232.

374 Cf., *mutatis mutandis*, EU Council Joint Action No. 2008/851/CFSP, Article 12.

375 See above, Part III, para. 1.

376 See, *mutatis mutandis*, ICJ, *Questions Relating to the Obligation to Prosecute or Extradite (Belgium v Senegal)*, judgment of July 20, 2012, para. 94.

377 Cf., as regards the transfer of pirates, House of Commons Foreign Affairs Committee, "Piracy off the coast of Somalia, Tenth Report of Session 2010-12," January 5, 2012, 54.

378 See above, Part II, para. 5.

379 See Council Framework Decision No. 2002/584/JHA, June 13, 2002, on the European arrest warrant and the surrender procedures between Member States 2002 *OJEU* L 190/1. See also Council Framework Decision No. 2009/299/JHA, February 26, 2009, amending Framework Decisions Nos. 2002/584/JHA, 2005/214/JHA, 2006/783/JHA, 2008/909/JHA and 2008/947/JHA, thereby enhancing the procedural rights of persons and fostering the application of the principle of mutual recognition to decisions rendered in the absence of the person concerned at the trial 2009 *OJEU* L 81/24.

sentence or detention order." The EAW is based on the principle of mutual recognition, which permits the transfer of suspected criminals who surrender without applying the complex extradition procedures which cause delays in prosecuting criminals and executing judicial decisions.[380] The EAW is an effective way to fight the transnational crime of smuggling migrants within the EU. However, if the activity should be undertaken entirely on the territory of a third country not belonging to the EU (or on the high seas), the principles of mutual recognition and mutual trust established within the EU legal system cannot be applied.[381]

More often, though, in the case of Operation *Sophia*, the Commander of the apprehending ship will simply hand the detainee over to the authorities of the State willing to exercise jurisdiction, together with property seized and evidence gathered.[382] This simplified procedure was expressly provided for by Article 12 Joint Action No. 2008/851/CFSP in the context of Operation *Atalanta* and it was also commonly followed in the framework of Operation *Ocean Shield* and by States participating in counter-piracy operations on an individual basis.[383]

The seizing authority, being bound by international human rights norms, must ensure that the transferred suspects will not be exposed to a serious risk of having their fundamental rights violated and must respect the prohibition of *refoulement*[384] under the ECHR[385] and the CFREU.[386]

Analogous concerns could arise in the event that the EU decides to conclude agreements for the transfer of suspected smugglers and traffickers captured within the framework of operations *Themis* and *Sophia* to Libya or other third

380 See again Council Framework Decision No. 2002/584/JHA, Article 1(2) and recital 5. For an in depth analysis of the principle of mutual recognition see, among others, ECJ, Case C-396/11, *Ciprian Vasile Radu*, judgment of January 29, 2013, para. 33 and Case C-42/11, *Lopes De Silva Jorge*, judgment of September 5, 2012, para. 28.

381 Ventrella, "The Impact," 12.

382 Cf. Giuseppe Licastro, "Brevi spunti (sulla base della documentazione disponibile) sull'azione di contrasto della Direzione nazionale antimafia ed antiterrorismo al *modus operandi* dei trafficanti di migranti," *La legislazione penale* (2018): 6–7.

383 See Enzo Mangini, "Caso Montecristo: la terza udienza contro i presunti pirati somali a Roma," June 27, 2012, http://www.lettera22.it/showart.php?id=12244&rubrica=122 (last accessed April 17, 2019).

384 Cf., among others, ECtHR, *Cruz Varas v Sweden*, Appl. No. 15576/89, judgment of March 20, 1991; HRC, General Comment No. 20, March 10, 1992, para. 9 and HRC, General Comment No. 31, March 29, 2004, para. 12. See above, Part II, para. 4.

385 Although the EU has not yet acceded to the ECHR, the latter's rules constitute general principles of EU Law under Article 6(3) TEU, and as such they bind both EU organs and Member States, when they implement their EU obligations.

386 Cf. Article 19(2) CFREU.

States that manifest an intention of subjecting them to criminal prosecution.[387] This issue has already emerged in relation to the efforts to combat maritime piracy.[388] In fact, the scant propensity shown by Member States to prosecute alleged pirates captured during Operation *Atalanta*[389] induced the EU to conclude agreements for the transfer of such individuals to third States.[390]

The agreements in question specified that the conditions for transfer to third States had to be consistent with respect for fundamental human rights, in order to ensure that no transferred individual would be subjected to the death penalty, acts of torture or cruel, inhuman or degrading treatments in that State.[391] However, this has not prevented issues of responsibility from arising in the case of transfers to States whose prison conditions did not meet the minimum requirements laid down in Article 3 ECHR.[392] The same may be said in the case of transfers to Libya because that State certainly cannot guarantee conditions of detention in conformity with international human rights standards and it is not in a position to conduct criminal proceedings consistent with the fair trial principle.

Part IV. National Strategies of Coastal States as Regards Migration Control Policy: the Case of Italy

Italy is the European State most pressed by migratory flows from Libya due to its geographical position in the Mediterranean. Italy's current strategy

---

387 See again in this regard Butler and Ratcovich, "Operation Sophia," 257.

388 On the issue, among others, cf. Annoni, "International," 189; Andrea Caligiuri, "La coopération régionale à l'épreuve de la repression pénale de la piraterie maritime," in *Stratégie logistique et de transport au service du développement en Afrique*, eds. Achaa Abdillahi Ahmed, Ibrahim Chitou and Bernadette Smeesters (Paris: L'Harmattan, 2015), 121.

389 See in this regard Treves, "Human Rights," 13.

390 See again Annoni, "International," 189 and Caligiuri, "La cooperation," 109.

391 For further references, see Treves, "Piracy," 399.

392 Verwaltungsgericht Köln, judgment of November 11, 2009, case No. 25 K 4280/09, www.justiz.nrw.de (last accessed April 18, 2019); for commentary see Anna Petrig, "Arrest, Detention and Transfer of Piracy Suspects: A Critical Appraisal of the German Courier Case Decision," in *Insecurity at Sea: Piracy and Other Risks to Navigation*, ed. Gemma Andreone *et al.* (Rome: Giannini, 2013), 153. Regarding the applicability of human rights norms in relation to EU military operations, particularly as regards the transfer of alleged pirates in the framework of Operation *Atalanta*: see generally Daniel Thym, "Transfer Agreements for Pirates Concluded by the EU. A Case Study on the Human Rights Accountability of the Common Security and Defence Policy," in *The Law and Practice of Piracy at Sea: European and International Perspectives*, eds. Panos Koutrakos and Achilles Skordas (Oxford: Hart, 2014), 167.

to counter human trafficking and migrant smuggling from North Africa is composite. First, with the full backing of the EU,[393] Italy has been trying to outsource its national border control to Africa. This is made possible through intense diplomatic activity aimed at intensifying cooperation with Libya and other African States.[394] As a result, Italy has obtained Libya's commitment to 'block' migrants within its borders on the basis of the model of cooperation already experimented with the Treaty of friendship, partnership and cooperation signed in Benghazi on August 30, 2008.[395]

At the same time, Italy has limited SAR activities carried out by NGOs in the Central Mediterranean through a variety of actions: the adoption of a code of conduct regulating the action of NGOs carrying out relief activities at sea;[396] increasingly intense criminalization of humanitarian activities at sea[397] and, finally, the concrete implementation of the national policy of 'closed harbors'.[398] These initiatives, taken as a whole, aim to reduce the flow of migrants to Italy and, consequently, to the EU, by closing off the Central Mediterranean route. However, they pose several problems with respect to the fundamental human rights of migrants.

1 *Italian Cooperation with Libya and Other African States*

Since the end of the Nineties, the Italian Government has concluded several cooperation agreements with African countries of origin and transit of migrants aimed at managing migratory flows. These include, for instance, the repatriation agreements concluded between Italy and Tunisia in 1998.[399] More recently, however, traditional international agreements have been replaced by agile and streamlined forms of partnership. Furthermore, notwithstanding

393 In 2015, with the European Agenda on Migration and the Valletta Action Plan, the EU inaugurated a new strategy aimed at reducing the influx of irregular migrants through interventions carried out outside the territory of the EU. This strategy is entrusted to the guidance of the Member States and implemented mainly through political acts. These instruments include the EU-Turkey Statement of March 2016 (on the issue see Chiara Favilli, "La cooperazione UE-Turchia per contenere il flusso dei migranti e richiedenti asilo: obiettivo riuscito?," *Diritti umani e diritto internazionale* 10 (2016): 405), as well as other instruments of cooperation and development aimed at combating irregular immigration to the EU.

394 See below, Part IV, para. 1.

395 See above, Introduction.

396 See below, Part IV, para. 2.

397 See below, Part IV, para. 3.

398 See below, Part IV, para. 4.

399 Cf. Francesca De Vittor, "Responsabilità degli Stati e dell'Unione europea nella conclusione e nell'esecuzione di 'accordi' per il controllo extraterritoriale della migrazione," *Diritti umani e diritto internazionale* 12 (2018): 11.

a specific obligation on the Italian Government to make public any international agreement not explicitly designated as a 'state secret',[400] in some cases these agreements have not been made public.[401] An example is the Memorandum concluded with Sudan in 2016,[402] and of the Cooperation Agreement with Niger, concluded in 2017.[403] In this framework, the Memorandum of Understanding between Italy and the Libyan Government of National Accord concluded in 2017 has assumed a crucial role.[404]

The aim of the Italian Government is to allow Libya to autonomously carry out actions to combat human trafficking and migrant smuggling in its own territory, including preventing smugglers from putting their ships to sea, and carrying out SAR operations in the maritime areas of its competence. Since 2017, in fact, on the basis of the Memorandum of Understanding, the Libyan Coast Guard, which is the national authority currently in charge of SAR activities in maritime areas of Libyan competence, has received vessels, financial support, and training from Italy and the EU.[405] In addition, Italy has dispatched some of its own war ships to Libyan territorial waters in order to support the Libyan

400 Regional administrative Tribunal, Appl. No. 5606/2018, judgment of November 16, 2018, www.asgi.it/wp-content/uploads/2018/11/sentenza-16-novembre-niger-foia.pdf (last accessed April 18, 2019).

401 On this issue see also Andrea Spagnolo, "Di intese segrete e alibi parlamentari: tra la decisione del TAR sull'accordo col Niger e il Global Compact sulle migrazioni," *SIDI Blog*, December 5, 2018.

402 Memorandum with Sudan, concluded on August 3, 2016, containing measures aimed at establishing a framework for cooperation to speed up repatriation procedures.

403 Cooperation Agreement with Niger, concluded in September 2017. It constitutes the legal basis for the bilateral support mission in the Republic of Niger authorized by the Italian Parliament in January 2018 and subsequently launched in September 2018; the aim of the mission is to increase the capacity to combat the illegal trafficking and threats to security in the context of a joint European and US effort to stabilize the area and strengthen the territorial control capabilities of the Nigerian authorities and the Sahel countries, to provide support for border and land surveillance activities and to limit the influx of migrants to Italian coasts.

404 Memorandum of Understanding between Italy and the Libyan Government of National Accord on Cooperation in the Field of Development, Fight against Illegal Immigration, Trafficking in Human Beings and Smuggling and on Enhancement of Border Security, Rome, February 2, 2017, http://itra.esteri.it/vwPdf/wfrm-RenderPdf.aspx?ID=50975. For further insights see Marina Mancini, "Italy's New Migration Control Policy: Stemming the Flow of Migrants from Libya without Regard for Their Human Rights," *Italian Yearbook of International Law* 27 (2017): 259.

405 For more detail, see Forensic Oceanography, "*Mare Clausum*: Italy and the EU's Undeclared Operation to Stem Migration across the Mediterranean," May 2018, www.osservatoriodiritti.it/wp-content/uploads/2018/05/italia-libia-report.pdf, 40–46 (last accessed April 26, 2019).

Coast Guard;[406] moreover, it supports and finances development programs in the Libyan regions affected by the phenomenon of irregular immigration. Furthermore, Italy has made substantial efforts to reinforce Libya's capacity to prevent the illegal entry of migrants headed to Italy through the Libyan southern border, in the belief that 'sealing off' Libya's southern border means sealing off Europe's southern border. The goal is to prevent departures from Libya or drastically reduce their number without being directly involved in operations that would otherwise expose Italy to condemnation for the violation of migrants' fundamental human rights.[407] However, it does not seem that these cooperation schemes have achieved the pursued goal: as noted, they raise several problems when it comes to guaranteeing respect for migrants' rights. The EU legislation imposes strict limitations on the choice of third countries with which to collaborate in preventing and combating irregular immigration.[408] This practice of non-selective outsourcing of border policing undermines the effectiveness of the international protection of human rights.[409]

A particularly problematic example in this respect is provided by activities carried out in the Mediterranean Sea by the Libyan Coast Guard in collaboration with the Italian MRCC. As said, States with coastlines facing each other and neighboring States usually enter into bilateral and multilateral agreements governing cooperation and coordination in their SAR activities.[410] These agreements are important to ensure that there is clarity as to who is responsible for the coordination of SAR incidents and that the transfer of such coordination from one authority to another runs smoothly.

However, no such formal agreement exists between Italy and Libya. Italy and Libya have substituted this standard formula for cooperation within the IMO framework with a rather unorthodox cooperative framework.[411] Italy has also used its MRCC to relay information concerning distress incidents occurring beyond the Italian official SRR off the Libyan coasts. Whilst officially conducting SAR activities at sea, the operations of the Libyan Coast Guard have practically had the effect of preventing migrants from leaving Libyan waters. Moreover, its activities are reported to have frequently limited the ability of private vessels, mainly of NGOs, to provide effective SAR services off the

406 Ibid., 48–49.

407 See again ECtHR, GC, *Hirsi Jamaa et al.*, para. 137.

408 Cf. Article 55 Regulation No. 2016/1624.

409 Cf. also Anna Liguori, *Migration Law and the Externalization of Border Controls. European State Responsibility* (London: Routledge, 2019).

410 See above, Part II, para. 3.

411 Kristof Gombeer and Melanie Fink, "Non-Governmental Organisations and Search and Rescue at Sea," *MarSafeLaw Journal* (2018): 8.

Libyan coast.[412] Thus, for instance, on September 26, 2017, the Libyan Coast Guard intercepted, on the high seas, the NGO vessel *Lifeline*, flying the Dutch flag, and transferred the migrants rescued by the *Lifeline* to a Coast Guard vessel headed to Libya.[413] On several occasions, NGOs have been at or near a scene of distress, but were given instructions by the Rome MRCC to leave their position or to refrain from providing assistance due to the expected arrival of the Libyan Coast Guard. This occurred, for instance, to the *Aquarius*, a vessel used by the NGO *SOS Méditerranée*, on November 23 and 24, 2017.[414]

2 The Italian Code of Conduct Regulating the Action of Non-Governmental Organizations Carrying Out Search and Rescue Activities at Sea

Along with the development of cooperation with Libya, Italy has drastically reduced its own SAR activities in the Mediterranean. The void left by the official authorities, in terms of SAR coverage in the Central Mediterranean since the completion of the Italian operation *Mare Nostrum*, was soon filled by civil society organizations undertaking private rescues. Especially since 2015, several NGOs have been carrying out privately funded SAR operations.[415] Whilst more NGOs became active in 2016, there was a substantial decline in 2017 due to pressure from and confrontations with public authorities.[416]

The activity of NGOs at sea has significantly changed the landscape of SAR activities in the Mediterranean. NGO vessels are in fact private ships but, unlike commercial vessels and fishing boats, they do not provide just occasional relief; rather, they are at sea for the specific purpose of helping people in distress. They consequently perform public functions of common interest similar to those performed by boats of State authorities in charge of the SAR service.[417] Indeed, NGO vessels sail continuously in waters where the greatest number of shipwrecks involving migrants occur, in order to provide prompt

412 On this issue, see further below, Part IV, paras. 2–3.

413 Steve Scherer, "Rescue Ship Says Libyan Coast Guard Shot at and Boarded It, Seeking Migrants," *Reuters*, Rome, September 26, 2017, www.reuters.com/article/us-europe-migrants-libya-ngo/rescue-ship-says-libyan-coast-guard-shot-at-andboarded-it-seeking-migrants-idUSKCN1C12I4 (last accessed April 18, 2019).

414 Cf., e.g., SOS-Méditerranée, "Woman Found Dead at Bottom of Rubber Boat after Rescue Operation in Central Mediterranean," November 24, 2017, www.sosmediterranee.com/press/woman-found-dead-at-bottom-of-rubber-boat-after-rescue-operation-in-central-mediterranean/ (last accessed April 18, 2019).

415 Daniela Irrera, "Migrants, the EU and NGOs: The 'Practice' of Non-Governmental SAR Operations," *Romanian Journal of European Affairs* 16 (2016), 28–30.

416 Forensic Oceanography, "*Mare Clausum*," 58–62. See further below, Part IV, para. 3.

417 Cf. again Irrera, "Migrants," 20.

aid to people in danger of drowning at sea. They are regularly contacted by the Italian MRCC and effectively replace State vessels that previously had the task of patrolling those areas to rescue people in danger at sea.

However, they do not enjoy the rights of government ships specifically provided for by the law of the sea.[418] In this respect, a regulatory gap can be found, because the rules codified in international instruments relating to the law of the sea are founded on a State-based view of the marine space and do not take into account the specific character of the rescue operations carried out by NGO vessels.[419]

During 2017, attempts were made to close the legislative gap by identifying the rules that should guide the action of NGOs during rescue activities in the Mediterranean. This effort resulted in the formulation of two different codes of conduct which are to some extent 'complementary'.[420] Both of them are intended to regulate, albeit unilaterally,[421] the participation of non-State actors in SAR activities: the first code was voluntarily drawn up by some NGOs active in the field of sea rescue,[422] and the second one was drafted by the Italian Government[423] and endorsed by the EU.[424]

The voluntary code of conduct of NGOs aims to create a shared framework of rules for the operational implementation of humanitarian principles guiding SAR operations and to establish shared work practices. The Code proposes a series of actions that NGOs should put in place during SAR operations in

---

418 For instance as regards immunity from the jurisdiction of other States under Articles 32 and 95 UNCLOS. See also ITLOS, *The 'ARA Libertad' Case* (*Argentina v Ghana*), Provisional Measures, Order of December 15, 2012, para. 95.

419 On the issue see Irini Papanicolopulu, "Immigrazione irregolare via mare, tutela della vita umana e organizzazioni non governative," *Diritto, Immigrazione e cittadinanza* 3 (2017): 22.

420 Ivi, 27.

421 For a critical view regarding the unilateral approach followed in the drafting of the codes of conduct, cf. again Papanicolopulu, "Immigrazione," 29.

422 Cf. Code of Conduct for Search and Rescue Operations undertaken by civil society Non-Governmental Organizations in the Mediterranean Sea, 2017, www.humanrightsatsea.org/wp-content/uploads/2017/03/20170302-NGO-Code-of-Conduct-FINAL-SECURED.pdf (last accessed April 18, 2019).

423 Code of Conduct for NGOs Involved in Migrant Rescue at Sea, Rome, August 7, 2017, www.interno.gov.it/sites/default/files/allegati/codice_condotta_ong.pdf (last accessed April 18, 2018).

424 Cf. "Press Statement Following Discussion on Central Mediterranean," Tallinn, July 6, 2017, www.eu2017.ee/news/press-releases/press-statement-following-discussions-central-mediterranean (last accessed April 18, 2019) and European Commission, "Action Plan on Measures to Support Italy, Reduce Pressure along the Central Mediterranean Route and Increase Solidarity," Brussels, July 4, 2017, SEC (2017) 339.

order to achieve the specified objectives. Particular importance is given to the commitment to cooperate in order to ensure maximum efficiency in rescue operations. The Code's content is binding exclusively to the extent that it reiterates binding rules of international law.[425]

Italy also tried to clarify the regulatory framework applicable to SAR operations conducted by NGOs through the elaboration of a Code of Conduct to which all NGOs operating in the Central Mediterranean were invited to subscribe. The main purpose of the Italian Code of Conduct is purportedly to guarantee the regular and effective conduct of rescue operations, in the interest of the rescued persons, those involved in the rescue operations, and the safety of navigation. However, according to some authors, the guidelines contained in the Italian Code of Conduct are actually aimed at inducing NGOs to decrease their efforts in SAR activities at sea.[426] More generally, legal commentators have highlighted the risk that the implementation of the Italian Code of Conduct could lead to omissions or deficiencies in relation to the rescue of migrants in the Central Mediterranean.[427]

Furthermore, its legal nature is not entirely clear: the most accredited view is that it is a unilateral declaration of domestic law.[428] The Italian Code of Conduct contains, in fact, a series of commitments that NGOs should voluntarily undertake upon subscribing to it. These commitments partly reflect similar obligations established by international law and the provisions of the Code at least partially seem to recognize the quasi-public function carried out by NGOs in the Mediterranean given the inertia of the Coastal States,[429] assigning them functions that are similar to those of law enforcement.[430] Indeed, the relief operations carried out by NGOs in recent years have often seen collaboration between the NGOs and the Italian MRCC, thus achieving the dual

425 For further considerations, cf. Papanicolopulu, "Immigrazione," 22–23.

426 Ivi, 26.

427 Federico Ferri, "Il Codice di condotta per le ONG e i diritti dei migranti: fra diritto internazionale e politiche europee," *Diritti umani e diritto internazionale* 12 (2018): 192.

428 In this regard see, among others, Gombeer and Fink, "Non-Governmental," 7–8; Martina Ramacciotti, "Sulla utilità di un codice di condotta per le organizzazioni non governative impegnate in attività di *search and rescue* (SAR)," *Rivista di diritto internazionale* 101 (2018): 214–215; Ferri, "Il Codice," 189.

429 See, e.g., the commitment to equip themselves with means and rely on personnel whose suitability and technical capabilities in mass rescue operations under all conditions are ascertained (point 13).

430 See, e.g., the commitment to recover, during the activities, once the migrants are rescued and, to the extent possible, the makeshift boats and the outboard engines used by the migrant smugglers/traffickers and to immediately inform the MRCC in Rome.

objective of saving human lives in danger at sea and enabling Italy to fulfill its obligations as a coastal State without having to rely on its own ships.[431]

The Italian Code of Conduct does not lay down specific sanctions in the event of non-compliance, but rather generically provides that failure to subscribe to it or non-compliance with the commitments set forth therein may result in the Italian authorities adopting measures addressed to the vessels concerned. A significant part of the commitments foreseen in the Code, however, appear to be problematic. On the one hand, it attributes to Italy competences which, under the law of the sea, belong to the flag State. For instance, it requires a commitment to declare, in accordance with the legislation of the flag State, to the competent authorities of the State where the NGO is registered, all sources of funding for their rescue activity at sea and to communicate, upon request, such information to the Italian authorities in compliance with the principle of transparency (point 11). On the other hand, the content of the commitments—often 'obscure'—does not correspond to applicable international law. This applies, for instance, in the case of the provision requiring NGOs to commit not to enter Libyan territorial waters, except in situations of grave and imminent danger requiring immediate assistance (point 1). According to a literal interpretation, it would seem that the provision arbitrarily limits the right of innocent passage enjoyed by all ships, including NGOs vessels engaged in rescue operations at sea, under Article 17 UNCLOS, which codifies a general rule of international law.[432] Moreover, the provision intended to prevent NGOs vessels from stationing in the Libyan territorial sea in order to provide relief appears to be in conflict with Article 18(2) UNCLOS, according to which a vessel may stop in the territorial sea of a third State as long as this is necessary for the purpose of rendering assistance to persons or ships in danger or distress.

Italy is not entitled to prohibit a ship flying the flag of a third State from entering Libyan territorial waters or from complying with the obligation to save people in distress at sea.[433] Indeed, the law of the sea does not give coastal States any powers to restrict foreign vessels' navigational rights in the territorial sea of other coastal States. Thus, any attempt to that effect by Italy, for example by committing NGOs, under the Italian Code of Conduct, not to enter Libyan territorial waters, has no basis under Article 3 of the SAR Convention. Again in reference to Libya, the same can be said with respect to the right of innocent

431 See above, Part II, para. 3.

432 Cf. Shabtai Rosenne and Louis Sohn (eds.), *United Nations Convention on the Law of the Sea. A Commentary* (Leiden: Nijhoff, 1982), 153.

433 On this issue see also Gombeer and Fink, "Non-Governmental," 9.

passage of ships flying the flag of a third State.[434] A coastal State has no legal grounds for preventing NGOs from conducting SAR activities in its own territorial sea. This is because entry to and presence in a State's territorial sea for the purpose of search and rescue operations does not render a vessel's passage non-innocent. Not only do NGOs have the right to navigate through territorial waters to save lives, but denying them access would infringe fundamental provisions of the UNCLOS and international human rights law. Even though Libya is not a party to the UNCLOS, the main tenets of the right to innocent passage as codified in the UNCLOS are considered to reflect customary international law, which Libya is bound to comply with.[435] Furthermore, in a human rights law perspective, prohibiting persons from exiting a State is generally not permitted because everyone is in principle free to leave any country, including their own.[436] On the other hand, the right to life imposes positive obligations on the coastal State to take adequate measures to prevent the deaths of those within its jurisdiction.[437] This equally applies in the context of SAR operations at sea.[438] Respecting and ensuring the right of migrants to be rescued entails an obligation to refrain from preventing the passage of NGO vessels in territorial waters when they are able to contribute to the prevention of the loss of life.[439]

Similar considerations also apply in relation to the commitment not to transfer the rescued persons to other ships, except in case of a request of the competent MRCC (point 7). Such a limitation cannot be found in any international treaty concerning rescue at sea[440] and it could violate the obligation of the ship's master to ensure the safety of rescued migrants and guarantee their

---

434 Ibid.

435 Cf. ICJ, *Case Concerning Military and Paramilitary Activities in and against Nicaragua (Nicaragua v United States of America)*, judgment of June 27, 1986, *ICJ Reports*, 1986, 214.

436 See above, Part II, para. 4.

437 See, among others, ECtHR, *Osman v The United Kingdom*, Appl. No. 23452/94, judgment of October 28, 1998, paras. 115–116 and *Kemaloğlu v Turkey*, Appl. No. 19986/06, judgment of April 10, 2012; cf. William Schabas, *The European Convention on Human Rights: A Commentary* (Oxford: OUP, 2015), 126–127.

438 See also ECtHR, *Leray v France*, Appl. No. 44617/98, judgment of January 16, 2001, where the ECtHR confirmed that the way in which maritime rescue operations are conducted is subject to judicial review in light of the right to life. See, among others, Lisa-Marie Komp, "The Duty to Assist Persons in Distress: An Alternative Source of Protection against the Return of Migrants and Asylum Seekers to the High Seas?," in *'Boat Refugees' and Migrants at Sea: A Comprehensive Approach*, eds. Violeta Moreno-Lax and Efthymios Papastavridis (Leiden: Nijhoff, 2016), 236–38.

439 On this subject, see also Gombeer and Fink, "Non-Governmental," 13–14.

440 To the contrary, the SAR regime urges coastal States to release assisting vessels from their obligations as soon as possible: see for example SAR Convention, section 3.1.9.

humane treatment.[441] Moreover, should the competent MRCC fail to request a transfer in the presence of a dangerous situation, Italy would bear responsibility for failing to ensure adequate, effective rescue operations. The transfer of people onto vessels other than that of the first NGO providing aid could in fact speed up conveyance to a safe place and allow the rescued persons to benefit from better transport conditions. In practice, NGO vessels engaged in rescue operations often provide life jackets, drinking water and urgent medical treatment and then transfer those they have rescued onto larger vessels of other NGOs[442] or even onto Italian military ships or other ships engaged in multilateral operations and endowed with a greater on-board capacity.

Further problems arise in relation to some rules requiring NGOs to actively cooperate in the investigation activities carried out by the police at the place of landing and aimed at the repression of migrant smuggling and human trafficking (point 12), including the commitment to receive on board, at the request of the competent Italian authorities, judicial police officers for information and evidence gathering (point 10).[443] These commitments are not without consequences for one of the fundamental principles of NGOs action: the independence of the NGOs from the Member States.[444]

Another problematic issue concerns the commitment foreseen by the Italian Code to cooperate with the competent MRCC, carry out its instructions and inform it in advance of any initiatives undertaken independently because deemed necessary and urgent (point 9). The coastal State can issue SAR instructions with a legally binding character on the high seas within its SRR.[445] Under international law, foreign private vessels are required to comply with SAR instructions issued by national authorities of the competent MRCC within its SRR. However, the commitment in the Italian Code of Conduct to follow the instructions of the competent MRCC can only be understood as applying in accordance with the duty to rescue people at sea. The SAR regime and human rights law, in fact, place legal limits on the permissible content of SAR instructions. A question arises in relation to problematic instructions NGOs have reportedly received in the recent past, when the national authorities instructed them to keep away from a distress scene, or to refrain from

441 See above, Part II, para. 3.

442 On this issue see Eugenio Cusumano, "Emptying the Sea with a Spoon? Non-Governmental Providers of Migrants Search and Rescue in the Mediterranean," *Marine Policy* 75 (2017), 92–94.

443 Cf. Ramacciotti, "Sulla utilità," 221.

444 Cf. Eugenio Cusumano, "Straightjacketing Migrant Rescuers? The Code of Conduct on Maritime NGOs," *Mediterranean Politics* 24 (2017).

445 *Contra* see Gombeer and Fink, "Non-Governmental," 15–16.

providing assistance, even though they were near or had already reached the distress scene,[446] or to bring migrants back to Libya. In all these cases, the SAR obligation is functional to safeguard life and therefore it prevails over conflicting instructions.

Furthermore, when multiple actors are present at a distress scene, preventing loss of life requires on-scene coordination in order to be effective.[447] The role of on-scene coordinator must be assigned to the first asset to arrive and to the most capable actor.[448] NGO crews typically have the operational expertise and capabilities to take on on-scene coordination responsibilities. In contrast, reports suggest that the Libyan Coast Guard does not possess the proper expertise to take on responsibility for on-scene coordination.[449] When the captain of an NGO vessel is appointed as on-scene coordinator for multiple SAR providers present, issuing counter-instructions or otherwise obstructing his or her coordination or execution is in breach of the SAR regime. Thus, for example, on November 6, 2017, the NGO Sea Watch arrived at a distress scene in response to a call from the Italian MRCC and assumed the on-scene coordination of all assets present in mutual agreement. However, when the Libyan Coast Guard arrived, it interrupted the on-scene rescue coordination and execution by the NGO. In the ensuing chaos, a number of persons drowned.[450] It is clear that instructions undermining effective on-scene coordination may violate the right to life of those in distress. As noted above, in fact, the right to life imposes positive obligations on States to take adequate measures to prevent deaths. In the present context, this means that a coastal State which should be aware of a danger to persons' lives (e.g. after a distress call), but gives instructions that are clearly detrimental to the chances of success of a rescue operation, would be violating human rights law whenever the distress scene is within its jurisdiction. Such a violation would occur when the distress scene is within the territorial sea of the coastal State or when the distress scene is on the high seas and international human rights apply in extraterritorial terms.[451] Thus, for instance, a number of incidents have been reported where the Libyan Coast Guard exercised coercion on NGO vessels in order to force their departure from a distress scene or to hand over rescued migrants. As mentioned earlier, such an incident occurred to the vessel *Lifeline* on September 26, 2017, when the

---

446 Cf. Gombeer and Fink, "Non-Governmental," 17–18.

447 The SAR Convention requires a clearly designated on-scene coordinator: cf. Section 4.7.

448 SAR Convention, Section 4.7.2.

449 Forensic Oceanography, "*Mare Clausum*," 57–81.

450 For a detailed account of the incident see again Forensic Oceanography, "*Mare Clausum*," 87–99.

451 On the issue see above, Part II, paras. 2–3.

Libyan Coast Guard fired shots into the water and air close to the NGO vessel, which had previously rescued a group of migrants and set course for Italy.[452]

Establishing human rights jurisdiction is more complicated when a coastal State's agents are not physically present at the distress scene on the high seas. Regarding this issue, some authors have argued that a nearby physical presence—even without using force—can constitute effective control.[453] Others have argued that being both aware of a situation and in a position to save lives triggers due diligence obligations, even when the traditional legal bases for jurisdiction are missing.[454] These arguments, however, have not yet been confirmed in human rights law adjudications. An interesting test case in this regard is the recent case brought against Italy before the ECtHR by seventeen survivors of the above mentioned incident of November 6, 2017, together with the NGO Sea Watch.[455]

3 *The Criminalization of Humanitarian Activities at Sea*

The intervention of NGOs in the Central Mediterranean has very much changed the landscape; according to official reports, they have performed as much as half of the total rescues undertaken.[456] This, in turn, has been perceived as creating a 'magnet effect' or 'pull factor', which serves both to encourage and facilitate the deeds of human traffickers and migrant smugglers.[457] In particular, Frontex has maintained that smugglers are able to adapt

452 See above, Part IV, para. 1.

453 Paolo Biondi, "Italy Strikes Back Again: A Push-Back's Firsthand Account," *Border Criminologies*, December 15, 2017. See also Violeta Moreno-Lax and Mariagiulia Giuffré, "The Raise of Consensual Containment: From 'Contactless Control' to 'Contactless Responsibility' for Forced Migration Flows," in *Research Handbook on International Refugee Law*, ed. Satvinder Singh Juss (London: Edward Elgar, 2019).

454 Vassilis Tzevelekos and Elena Katselli Proukaki, "Migrants at Sea: A Duty of Plural States to Protect (Extraterritorially)?," *Nordic Journal of International Law* 86 (2017): 427, 455 and 463.

455 Global Legal Action Network, "Legal Action against Italy over Its Coordination of Libyan Coast Guard Pull-Backs Resulting in Migrant Deaths and Abuse," May 8, 2018, www.glanlaw.org/single-post/2018/05/08/Legal-action-against-Italy-over-its-coordination-of-Libyan-Coast-Guard-pull-backs-resulting-in-migrant-deaths-and-abuse (last accessed April 27, 2019); cf. also Moritz Baumgärtel, "High Risk, High Reward: Taking the Question of Italy's Involvement in Libyan 'Pullback' Policies to the European Court of Human Rights," *EJIL: Talk!*, May 14, 2018.

456 EUNAVFOR MED Operation Sophia—Six Monthly Report, January 1/October 31, 2016, Council Doc. 14978/16, November 30, 2016, 7–8.

457 Demonstrating the baselessness of this assertion, see Elias Steinhilper and Rob Gruijters, "Border Deaths in the Mediterranean: What We Can Learn from the Latest Data," *Border Criminologies Blog*, March 8, 2017.

their routes on the basis of where SAR operations take place.[458] Furthermore, the joint communication adopted by the European Commission and the High Representative for Foreign Affairs and Security Policy, on the management of migrant flows and on the safeguarding of lives in the Central Mediterranean, focused attention on NGO SAR activities with reference to their operating area or the activities carried out near the Libyan coasts.[459]

The doubt was raised that rescue activities in the maritime areas closest to Libya would change the traffickers' *modus operandi*, inducing them to embark migrants on dinghies completely unsuitable for navigation and with which there was no possibility of being able to reach the Italian coasts, as they could count on relief efforts near the Libyan territorial sea or even inside it,[460] thus effectively facilitating the business of smugglers and traffickers.[461] These suspicions have since translated into a number of charges against NGOs in several EU Member States.

In Italy, in explicit reference to the allegations launched by Frontex,[462] several investigations were opened into the alleged 'collusion' between NGOs and Libyan traffickers.[463] Following investigations carried out by a Sicilian Public Prosecutor's Office, the suspicion spread that some NGOs active along the Central Mediterranean route were responsible for encouraging irregular

458 See Frontex, "Risk Analysis for 2016," March 2016, www.frontex.europa.eu/assets/Publications/Risk_Analysis/Annula_Risk_Analysis_2016.pdf, 39.

459 European Commission and High Representative of the Union for Foreign Affairs and Security Policy, Joint Communication to the European Parliament, the European Council and the Council, "Migration on the Central Mediterranean Route Managing Flows, Saving Lives," Brussels, January 25, 2017, Doc. JOIN(2017) 4 final, 6.

460 Ibid., 6.

461 Frontex Agency Director, interview with the German newspaper Die Welt: Manuel Bewarder and Lisa Walter, "Rettungseinsätze vor Libyen müssen auf den Prufstand," *Die Welt*, February 27, 2017, www.welt.de/politik/deutschland/article162394787/Rettungseinsaetze-vor-Libyen-muessen-auf-den-Pruefstand.html (last accessed April 18, 2019).

462 Cfr. Alessandra Ziniti, "Migranti, sulle Ong Zuccaro insiste: Notizie date da Frontex, non ho nuove prove," *la Repubblica*, May 3, 2017, available at: www.repubblica.it/cronaca/2017/05/03/news/ong_migranti_scafisti_procura_catania_zuccaro-164500643/ (last accessed April 18, 2019).

463 These concerns had clearly emerged in the remarks presented to the Senate Defense Committee by the Director of Frontex and the Prosecutor in Chief of Catania: cf. Italian Senate Defence Committee, Document approved by the fourth permanent Commission at the conclusion of the fact-finding survey on the contribution of Italian soldiers to the control of migratory flows in the Mediterranean and the impact of the activities of non-governmental organizations, May 16, 2017, Doc. XVII No. 9, www.senato.it/japp/bgt/showdoc/frame.jsp?tipodoc=SommComm&leg=17&id=01022634&part=doc_dc-sedetit_pi-genbl_icscdmiacdfmnmeli&parse=no (last accessed April 18, 2019).

immigration to Italy or even providing help to those responsible for migrant smuggling and human trafficking.

In several instances, the master and crew of a vessel that had saved people at sea and successively disembarked them in an Italian harbor were charged with violating Italian domestic laws on the prohibition of illegal migration or even on other counts.[464] The same fate has also been suffered by migrants rescued at sea and disembarked in an Italian harbor.

As far back as 2004, the German NGO vessel *Cap Anamur*, after having saved thirty-seven people in the Mediterranean, had to moor for twenty-one days on the high seas close to the outer limit of Italian territorial waters, before being allowed to call at an Italian port. The crew of the *Cap Anamur*, after being arrested for facilitating the illegal entry of migrants into Italian territory, were eventually released and fully acquitted by the Agrigento Court in 2009.[465]

An interesting case is that of the vessel *Open Arms* belonging to the NGO Proactiva Open Arms, whose rescue ship was impounded by the Italian authorities on March 27, 2018[466] and later released on April 16, 2018.[467] The captain of the ship and some other members of the crew of the Spanish NGO were investigated for criminal association[468] and aiding irregular immigration.[469]

On March 15, 2018, the Italian MRCC informed the *Open Arms* of the presence of a dinghy travelling on international waters off the Libyan coast. The *Open Arms* was heading towards it when the Libyan Coast Guard took over the coordination of the SAR operations and ordered the NGO vessel to stay out of sight.[470] However, when it arrived near the scene of the incident, the *Open Arms* did not see the Libyan Coast Guard vessel and decided to proceed with

464 Thus, for instance, some members of the NGO *Médecins sans Frontières* were investigated for alleged illegal disposal of a large quantity of dangerous waste posing an infectious risk; the waste was claimed to have been dumped by the *Aquarius* and *Vos Prudence* vessels between January 2017 and May 2018. Recently, however, this line of inquiry as well proved to be devoid of any foundation.

465 Regarding this case and the decisions of the Italian judges, see Marco Cottone, "Alcune notazioni in materia di reati connessi all'immigrazione clandestina via mare," in *L'immigrazione irregolare via mare nella giurisprudenza italiana e nell'esperienza europea*, ed. Tullio Scovazzi *et al.* (Turin: Giappichelli, 2016), 90.

466 Tribunal of Catania, Decree of validation and preventive seizure, March 27, 2018, www.questionegiustizia.it (last accessed April 18, 2019).

467 Tribunal of Ragusa, Decree rejecting a request for preventive seizure, April 16, 2018 and Tribunal of Ragusa, Order to confirm the decree of the pre-trial judge, May 11, 2018, www.questionegiustizia.it (both last accessed April 18, 2019).

468 Article 416 Italian Criminal code.

469 Article 12 Legislative Decree No. 286/1998.

470 Tribunal of Ragusa, Decree rejecting a request for preventive seizure, April 16, 2018, 3.

the rescue operations. It then sailed towards a second dinghy that had been spotted in the meantime; while embarking people from this second boat, the Libyan Coast Guard arrived and ordered the NGO vessel not to approach the migrants. The *Open Arms* crew, after ascertaining the inaction of the Libyan Coast Guard, still managed to complete the rescue of the people from the second dinghy and headed north, in search of a 'place of safety' where it could disembark the migrants. A third inflatable boat was instead intercepted by the Libyans and the migrants who occupied it were disembarked in Libya. The *Open Arms* reached the Italian coast and was authorized to disembark the rescued people in Pozzallo, in Sicily. Shortly after the safe landing, the NGO was informed that the Catania Prosecutor had issued an order to impound the vessel and charged some members of the *Open Arms*' crew with belonging to a criminal organization and smuggling migrants.[471]

The order for the pre-trial seizure of the *Open Arms* vessel focused on whether it was plausible to assume that the defendants had committed a crime. In particular, the judge examined whether the conduct of the *Open Arms* crew, which had refused to hand over the migrants to the Libyan authorities and had brought them to Italy, should be considered migrant smuggling. For its own part, the NGO argued that the crew had acted out of necessity, citing Article 54 of the Italian Criminal Code ('state of necessity') in their defense: the unlawful conduct was to be considered as justified because of the necessity to protect rescued migrants from a current danger of a serious harm. On the one hand, the pre-trial judge noted that the migrants were not in imminent danger because their dinghies, despite being overcrowded, were not leaking, the weather conditions were good and the Libyan Coast Guard was ready to intervene. On the other hand, however, the judge also stated that the *Open Arms* could not be obliged to hand over the migrants to the Libyan authorities because Libya could not be considered a 'safe place' for landing.[472] As a consequence, as long as the situation remained unchanged, the refusal of the members of the NGO to hand over the migrants to the Libyan authorities and the decision to bring them to Italy is justified.

The same solution was recently adopted also by the Tribunal of Trapani in the case *Vos Thalassa*.[473] On May 23, 2019, the Tribunal of Trapani acquitted two individuals who were rescued by the Italian-flagged tugboat *Vos Thalassa*, along with 65 other migrants, in the Sicilian Channel in July 2018. The two

471 For a detailed description of the facts, see De Vittor, "Soccorso," 443–453.

472 See again Tribunal of Ragusa, Decree rejecting a request for preventive seizure, April 16, 2018, 3.

473 Tribunal of Trapani, Decision No. 112 of May 23, 2019, https://www.asylumlawdatabase.eu/sites/default/files/aldfiles/GIP-Trapani%20%281%29.pdf (last accessed May 26, 2019).

defendants were arrested upon disembarkation in Italy for aiding illegal immigration and having threaten and coerced the *Vos Thalassa* crew while preventing to be returned to Libya. The judge held that the actions of the defendants were lawful in that they were acts of self-defence. The SAR incident occurred within the Libyan SRR and the authorities of that State took the responsibility of SAR operations by instructing the *Vos Thalassa* master to head towards Libya. The Tribunal held that the defendants were the victims of a wrongful and their reaction was proportionate in the context of the circumstances of the case, given that in Libya the fundamental rights of the applicants, including their right to life and to personal integrity, were at stake.

The same conclusion was accepted also by the Tribunal of Agrigento in the case *Sea Watch 3*.[474] On June 26, 2019, after having rescued 53 persons in the Libyan SRR and having spent fifteen days off Lampedusa, the master of the ship, due to the critical conditions of migrants on board, decided to enter the Italian territorial waters, thus violating the formal measure by which the Italian Government prohibited the vessel to enter, transit or stop in the territorial sea of that State. On June 29, 2019, the master of the ship decided to enter the Italian harbor to disembark migrants and she was investigated for resistance and violence against public officials for not having complied with the order to stop and for having hit an Italian patrol boat while docking. The judge held that the conduct of the captain was legitimate in that it was an act of fulfillment of the duty to rescue persons in danger at sea. Libya, in fact, cannot be considered a safe place for disembarkation of migrants and the rescue operations can only be considered to end with the landing of migrants in a safe place. The judge also established that the Decree Law giving the Italian Minister of the Interior the faculty of adopting formal measures limiting or prohibiting ships engaged in the discharge of persons in violation of the laws of the State, the entry, transit or stop in the territorial sea and providing for economic sanctions and the possibility of seizing the ship in case of reiteration of the conduct,[475] was not applicable as regards vessels engaged in SAR activities at sea because their actions cannot be considered a threat for public security.

Both the pre-trial order in the *Open Arms* case, later confirmed by the Tribunal, and the decisions adopted by the Tribunal of Trapani in the case *Vos Thalassa* and by the Tribunal of Agrigento in the case *Sea Watch 3* are laudable

474 Tribunal of Agrigento, Decision No. 2592 of July 2, 2019, https://dl-iusondemand.s3.amazonaws.com/ricercagiuridica.com/rackete-ordinanza-rigetto.pdf (last accessed July 3, 2019).

475 Cf. Decree Law No. 53 of June 14, 2019, "Urgent provisions on public order and security," entered into force on June 19, 2019, Official Gazette No. 138, June 14, 2019.

because they provide an interpretation of the concept of 'place of safety' that is in line with international human rights law. Furthermore, the decisions recognize the right of all migrants not to be delivered to a place where they risk being exposed to the treatments prohibited by Article 3 ECHR. This is important, as it contrasts with the common belief that only refugees have the right not to be deported back to Libya, while 'economic migrants' can be pushed back. In this respect, the decisions take a step forward compared to the ECtHR decision in the case of *Hirsi Jamaa*, where the ECtHR condemned Italy for its 'push-back' operations to Libya because the applicants were all in need of international protection.[476]

Furthermore, the Tribunal of Ragusa clarified what constituted the offense of facilitating illegal immigration under Article 12 Legislative Decree No. 286/1998 and on what basis it should be ruled out in the case of the NGO staff operating in the Mediterranean.[477] First of all, commission of the crime is conditional on fulfilment of the subjective element consisting in the awareness of promoting, directing, organizing, financing or carrying out illegal transport of foreigners into the territory of the State or performing other acts aimed at illegally procuring entry into the territory of the State. Moreover, the crime is not committed in the absence of any agreement or collaboration with smugglers who organize departures from Libya, or when the rescue operation is conducted while maintaining constant communication with the Italian MRCC and a landing is made with the authorization of the Italian authorities and in the place indicated by them.[478] In fact, rescue operations only end with the landing of migrants in a safe place. Consequently, the transport of migrants to the 'place of safety' designated by the competent MRCC must be considered such as a part of the rescue obligation. The same still holds true even when the landing is made without the authorization of the Italian authorities such as in the case of the NGO vessel *Sea Watch 3*. This interpretation appears to be the only one compatible with applicable international obligations binding Italy, and precisely with Articles 3 and 6 Smuggling Protocol and the customary rule on the duty to rescue people found in danger at sea codified under the UNCLOS.[479]

476 Cf. ECtHR, GC, *Hirsi Jamaa et al.*, para. 125. For further considerations see Virginia Passalacqua, "The 'Open Arms' Case: Reconciling the Notion of 'Place of Safety' with the Human Rights of Migrants," *EJIL: Talk!*, May 21, 2018.

477 Tribunal of Ragusa, Order of confirmation of the decree of the pre-trial judge, May 11, 2018.

478 On the issue see also De Vittor, "Soccorso," 451–452.

479 See above, Part II, para. 3.

4 *The Italian Policy of 'Closed Harbors'*

Although a formal decision to close the harbors has never been adopted until June 2019, since June 2017 the 'closure' of Italian harbors to NGOs involved in relief activities in the Central Mediterranean has been proposed by the Italian Government on several occasions to deny the disembarkation of migrants rescued at sea.[480] In its early stages, the 'threat' not to allow the landing of people rescued at sea in Italian harbors served a dual purpose. On the one hand, the government aimed to obtain greater logistic and financial support from the EU by virtue of the solidarity obligations set forth under Article 80 TFEU. On the other hand, it sought to pressure the European Commission into imposing the quotas established by decisions No. 1523/2015[481] and No. 1601/2015[482] for the relocation of persons in need of international protection on all Member States.

Starting from June 2018, however, given the continued inaction of both the European Institutions and Member States, the Italian Government ordered the 'closure' of Italian harbors to ships engaged in rescue activities in the Mediterranean, and in particular, but not exclusively, to NGOs flying the flag of a third State. Since then, several episodes have occurred off the Italian coast regarding SAR activities conducted both under the coordination of the Italian MRCC, as for example in the case of the *Aquarius*, which will be discussed shortly below, and under the formal coordination of the Libyan Coast Guard, such as in the *Open Arms* case discussed earlier.[483]

On the night of June 9, 2018, 629 migrants were rescued during a SAR operation carried out by the *Aquarius*, a rescue vessel operated by the Franco-German NGO SOS Méditerranée flying the flag of Gibraltar. The *Aquarius* was on its

480 Cf. the statements made by the Italian representative to the EU, Maurizio Massari, to the competent European Commissioner, Dimitris Avramopoulos: Steve Scherer and Gabriela Baczynska, "Italy Pleads to EU for Help with Migrants, Threatens to Close Ports," *Reuters*, June 28, 2017.

481 Council Decision No. 2015/1523, September 14, 2015, establishing provisional measures in the area of international protection for the benefit of Italy and Greece, L 239/146, September 15, 2015.

482 Council Decision No. 2015/1601, September 22, 2015, establishing provisional measures in the area of international protection for the benefit of Italy and Greece, L 248/80, September 24, 2015 (no longer in force since September 26, 2017).

483 The vessel *Open Arms* asked the Italian MRCC to indicate a safe haven for the disembarkation of rescued migrants. However, the Italian Government replied that since the rescue had taken place in waters of Libyan SAR competence and under the coordination of the Libyan Coast Guard, the MRCC would not assume responsibility for identifying a place for the disembarkation and the *Open Arms* would have to contact its own flag State. Thus, a bilateral negotiation between Italian and Spanish authorities began. Cf. De Vittor, "Soccorso," 444 and see above, Part IV, para. 3.

way to Italy when, at around 35 nautical miles off the southern coast of Italy, the Italian authorities ordered the *Aquarius* to stop. Italy refused access to its harbors and prohibited disembarkation of the rescued migrants on Italian territory. For another 24 hours, the *Aquarius* remained on stand-by, floating between Malta and Italy. Maltese and Italian vessels supplied the *Aquarius* with water and food, but neither country offered the migrants safe haven. The impasse was only solved on June 11, when Spain allowed the *Aquarius* to dock in the port of Valencia. When it appeared that this journey would be too dangerous for both the migrants and the *Aquarius* crew and the Valencia plan seemed off the table again, Italy offered its ships to facilitate safe passage to Spain.[484] Just ten days after the *Aquarius* incident, another similar episode of denial of access to ports by Italy occurred, after the Dutch-flagged ship of the German NGO Mission Lifeline rescued hundreds of migrants off the coast of Libya.[485]

The *Aquarius* and analogous cases raise a broad variety of questions, the most important of which being to assess whether Italy is violating international law by not allowing NGOs vessels to find a safe haven in one of its ports. The question is even more problematic following the entry into force of the Decree Law No. 53 of June 14, 2019, giving the Italian Minister of the Interior the faculty of adopting formal measures limiting or prohibiting vessels engaged in the discharge of persons in violation of the laws of the State, the entry, transit or stop in the territorial sea.[486] General international law assigns States the power to regulate entry into the territories over which they exercise their sovereignty, including their respective harbors.[487] This means that, in principle, no State is obliged to allow foreign vessels into its ports, except where this is provided for under a bilateral or multilateral treaty or in cases of distress or *force majeure*.[488]

On the one hand, treaty provisions on SAR activities at sea which are binding for Italy do not constitute an obligation to allow access to Italian harbors to the vessels that have carried out the rescue of migrants at sea. The SOLAS and SAR Conventions, in fact, do not establish specific provisions as regards the landing of rescued persons. The State coordinating rescue operations

484 For a detailed description of the facts see Melanie Fink and Kristof Gombeer, "The Aquarius Incident: Navigating the Turbulent Waters of International Law," *EJIL: Talk!*, June 14, 2018.

485 Cf. http://www.ansa.it/english/news/2018/06/21/govt-attacks-illegal-ngo-migrant-rescue-off-libya-3_5349ce67-a761-4ca0-a3b5-832f0aa98fb3.html (last accessed April 18, 2019).

486 Cf. above, Part IV, para. 3.

487 Alan Lowe, "The Right of Entry into Maritime Ports in International Law," *San Diego Law Review* 14 (1977).

488 Churchill and Lowe, *The Law of the Sea*, 63.

is not also obliged to accept ships in its own harbors; it only has the main responsibility for identifying a safe landing place, which can be reached without exposing the people on board the ship to any risks.[489] On the other hand, however, the situation of extreme danger which both the NGO crew and people rescued at sea might risk finding themselves in could be qualified as a case of distress[490] in the event that their life or physical integrity is threatened. As a consequence the flag State could not be accused of committing a wrongful act if the captain of the ship decides to enter the harbor, despite the coastal State's denial of authorization.[491] However, even in that case, Italy could still deny access to the NGO vessel and limit itself to providing immediate and sufficient medical assistance to the persons in distress on board the vessel: the coastal State is not strictly obligated to grant access to the vessel as such if the life of the people on board is no longer at risk.[492]

The closure of Italian ports is not without consequences also in terms of compliance with international standards on human rights law and refugee protection. The situation, however, is complex. As seen, States have human rights obligations only towards individuals who find themselves within their respective jurisdictions and, possibly, within their respective SRR. As a consequence, ships that are given an order not to enter the harbor while they are in the Italian territorial sea are certainly *de jure* under Italian jurisdiction and the order can be regarded as a violation of the rescued people's human rights,[493] in particular their rights under Articles 2 and 3 ECHR, to the extent that those rescued are in need of urgent medical care and/or lack basic necessities, and their needs cannot be met due to the denial of access to the harbors of the coastal State. Furthermore, the denial of access to Italian ports, insofar as it precludes an assessment of the individual situations of the persons concerned, could violate the prohibition of collective expulsions established under Article 4 Protocol No. 4 ECHR,[494] the principle of *non-refoulement*,[495] and also the *erga*

489 See above, Part II, para. 3.

490 The SAR Convention defines the distress phase as a situation wherein there is a reasonable certainty that a person, a vessel or other craft is threatened by grave and imminent danger and requires immediate assistance: cf. Annex, para. 1.3.13.

491 On this issue see, among others, Ferri, "Il Codice," 193.

492 Cf. also Efthymios Papastavridis, "The Aquarius Incident and the Law of the Sea: Is Italy in Violation of the Relevant Rules?," *EJIL: Talk!*, June 27, 2018.

493 See also De Sena and De Vittor, "La 'minaccia'," 4.

494 See again ECtHR, GC, *Hirsi Jamaa et al.*, paras. 159–186; GC, *Khlaifia et al. v Italy*, Appl. No. 16483/12, judgment of December 15, 2016; *N.D. and N.T. v Spain*, Appl. No. 8675/15, judgment of October 3, 2017.

495 Moreover, if the vessels are in Italian territorial waters, the denial of access to the Italian harbor would be incompatible with Directive No. 2013/32, whose application must also be

omnes obligation to guarantee access to precise procedures for obtaining refugee status.

However, Italian ports have also been closed to Italian-flagged military vessels. By way of example, it is worth mentioning two different contentious cases involving the *Ubaldo Diciotti*, an Italian-flagged ship, which occurred between July and August 2018. In both cases, the ship was anchored in Sicily without receiving the authorization to disembark the migrants onboard. The Italian Government authorized the disembarkation only after an agreement had been reached with other States for the distribution of incoming migrants on a voluntary basis.[496] In a human rights law perspective, the migrants were blocked on board the vessel for days in violation of their individual right to personal freedom.[497] Italian jurisdiction over the migrants on board was clearly established. It is a well-established rule of customary international law that a vessel is subject to the jurisdiction of its flag State,[498] and the flag State's jurisdiction also extends to the persons on board the ship.[499] Furthermore, State officials were physically present aboard the vessel, so the migrants on board were under the *de jure* and *de facto* control of the State.[500] However, it is not fully clear on what legal basis, either at the international or national level, migrants may be deprived of their liberty and whether there exists a sufficient, precise procedure prescribed by law on this point. The Italian Government did not specify the grounds on which it ordered the detention, nor did it produce a detention order, which in Italy may be issued only by judicial authorities.[501] Therefore, the period of detention on board inflicted upon the migrants does not seem to be compatible with the guarantees provided by Article 5 ECHR.[502]

The situation is more complex as regards NGOs vessels receiving an order not to access a harbor coastal State while they still are on the high seas, as in the case of the *Aquarius*. In a situation of this kind, as mentioned, States

guaranteed in the territorial sea of the State (Article 3): cf. again De Sena and De Vittor, "La 'minaccia'," 4.

496 For a detailed description of the facts of the case see Francesca Mussi, "The Italian Job: Human Rights Considerations of the Diciotti Incident," *Rights!*, October 18, 2018.

497 See above, Part II, para. 5.

498 See Article 92 UNCLOS.

499 Cf. ITLOS, *The M/V 'Saiga' Case No. 2*, para. 106.

500 See above, Part II, para. 2.

501 Cf. Tribunal of Catania, section for crimes of Ministers, judgment of January 23, 2019, available at: http://www.senato.it (last accessed June 24, 2019), 24–25.

502 See again above, Part II, para. 5.

are considered to exercise jurisdiction when State officials are physically present at the scene of a particular incident and thus exercise effective control over the individuals seeking protection.[503] Accordingly, had Italian State vessels sailed to the high seas to physically prevent the *Aquarius* from approaching its territorial sea, the persons on board the *Aquarius* would have found themselves within its *de facto* jurisdiction. Thus, for instance, where entry into the harbor was militarily prevented by the Italian Coast Guard, the persons involved would fall under Italian jurisdiction, pursuant to Article 1 ECHR.[504]

In this specific case, however, Italian agents were not physically present on the high seas and, as said, it was not easy to establish Italian jurisdiction. In particular, by instructing the *Aquarius* to stand by, Italy indisputably exercised some control over it. However, it is unclear whether this control was sufficient to bring the persons on board the *Aquarius* within Italy's *de facto* jurisdiction. Whilst the relevance of SAR instructions for the purposes of establishing jurisdiction has yet to be determined by the ECtHR, some clarifications in this regard may come from the recent case brought against Italy in connection with the SAR incident taking place on November 6, 2017.[505]

Thus, as the law currently stands, the decision by Italy to close its harbors to the *Aquarius* and other NGOs ship engaged in SAR activities in the Central Mediterranean does not manifestly breach human rights law unless the NGO ship is in distress, as in the case of *Sea Watch 3* and *Sea Eye*. From December 22, 2018, for 19 days, 49 migrants were kept on board the vessels *Sea Watch 3* and *Sea Eye*, respectively flying the German and Dutch flags, on the high seas off Malta, waiting to receive an indication of a safe haven. Only after an agreement was reached for the redistribution of migrants among several European countries was the 'crisis' eventually resolved. For this reason, pending negotiations, Malta granted the two vessels the permission to enter its territorial sea to seek refuge from the storm and to receive supplies and aid.[506]

503 See above, Part II, para. 2 and Part IV, para. 2.

504 In the *Women on Waves* case the ECtHR determined that the prohibition imposed on the Dutch ship *Borndiep*, which was denied entry to Portuguese territorial waters, constituted an exercise of jurisdiction under Article 1 ECHR: see ECtHR, *Women on Waves v Portugal*, Appl. No. 31276/05, judgment of February 3, 2009, paras. 9 and 22.

505 See again above, Part IV, para. 2.

506 Cf. www.infomigrants.net/en/post/14477/migrants-rescued-by-sea-watch-3-and-sea-eye-speak-out (last accessed April 27, 2019).

Part v. International Responsibility for Human Rights Violations Perpetrated in Connection with Counter-Smuggling and Counter-Trafficking Operations

1 *International Responsibility for Human Rights Violations in the Context of Naval Operations at Sea*

Numerous States and international organizations take part in operations aimed at combating migrant smuggling by sea through the Central Mediterranean.[507] This makes it necessary to assess some issues related to the attribution of responsibility for possible violations of fundamental human rights committed in the course of maritime operations.

Although the operations in the area were authorized by the Security Council, the Council does not exercise powers of direction or control as far as the activities of the forces involved are concerned. Moreover, as mentioned, each of these forces possesses its own chain of command;[508] accordingly, any wrongful conduct engaged in by such forces—including those of the EU—cannot, as a rule, be attributed to the UN.[509]

However, in order to establish whether NATO and the EU may be held responsible for the wrongful acts of the national contingents that participate, respectively, in the *Sea Guardian* mission and in operations *Themis* and *Sophia*, it is above all necessary to verify whether the two international organizations are endowed with legal personality under international law. Although some legal scholars consider NATO to be an international entity that enjoys autonomy from its Member States,[510] various elements of international practice suggest the opposite, i.e. that NATO is a joint organ of States.[511] In such a case, the wrongful conduct of military contingents taking part in the *Sea Guardian* operation should be attributed exclusively to the sending States.[512]

---

507 See above, Part I, para. 1.

508 See again above, Part I, para. 1.

509 Cf., *mutatis mutandis*, ECtHR, *Al-Jedda v The United Kingdom*, Appl. No. 27021/08, judgment of July 7, 2011. For commentary, see Francesco Messineo, "Things Could Only Get Better: Al-Jedda Beyond Behrami," *Military Law and the Law of War Review* 50 (2011) 321.

510 See generally Giuseppe Cassoni, *L'Organizzazione del Trattato dell'Atlantico del Nord* (Milan: Giuffrè, 1967), 23 and, more recently, Zwanenburg, *Accountability*, 64.

511 Tarcisio Gazzini, "NATO's Role in the Collective Security System," *Journal of Conflict and Security Law* 8 (2003): 240.

512 Regarding the operations carried out in the Mediterranean in 2011, see Charles Heller and Lorenzo Pezzani, "Report on the 'Left-To-Die Boat,'" 2012, www.fidh.org/IMG/pdf/fo-report.pdf (last accessed April 18, 2019) and Efthymios Papastavridis, "Rescuing 'Boat People' in the Mediterranean Sea: The Responsibility of States under the Law of the Sea," *EJIL: Talk!*, May 31, 2011.

The EU is a different matter, as its legal personality under international law no longer appears to be under dispute.[513] However, a distinction must be made in this respect between EU missions carried out in the context of Frontex and EU military operations.

The regime of responsibility arising in the case of military missions launched by the EU has been broadly debated in the literature.[514] More precisely, it is a matter of establishing whether the State taking part in the operations or the EU should be held answerable for wrongful acts committed by a national contingent assigned to the mission, or whether there exists a regime of joint responsibility between the EU and the States participating in the mission.

In this regard, as previously said, the DARIO establishes that the conduct of an organ of a State placed at the disposal of an international organization must be considered an act of the organization where the latter exercises effective control over the conduct in question.[515] In the case of Operation *Sophia*, as noted earlier, the multinational forces operate under a common chain of command headed by the Commander of the operation designated by the EU. The ROE, operational programme and chain of command are all established by the Political and Security Committee, which is responsible for the strategic direction and political control of the operation, under the responsibility of the Council of the EU and the High Representative of the EU.[516] Moreover, Council Decision No. 2015/778 acknowledges that Operation *Sophia* has the nature of an EU military operation[517] and any SOFA agreements with Libya and other North African States must be directly negotiated by the EU itself, not the single Member States participating in the mission.[518]

513 Cf. Article 47 TEU; Philippe Gautier, "The Reparation for Injuries Case Revisited: The Personality of the European Union," *Max Planck Yearbook of United Nations Law* 4 (2000): 331; Pieter Jan Kuijper *et al.* (ed.), *The Law of EU External Relations: Cases, Materials and Commentary on the EU as an International Actor* (Oxford: OUP, 2013), 1 and Frederik Naert, "The International Responsibility of the Union in the Context of its CSDP Operations," in *The International Responsibility of the European Union. European and International Perspectives*, ed. Malcolm D. Evans (Oxford: Hart, 2013), 313.

514 On this issue see generally Naert, "The International Responsibility," 313 and Sari and Wessel, "International Responsibility," 126. See above, Part I, para. 4.

515 See again Article 7 DARIO. See above, Part I, para. 4.

516 See above, Part I, paras. 2 and 4.

517 Decision No. 2015/778/CFSP, Article 1.

518 Ibid., Article 10. See in this regard Panos Koutrakos, "International Agreements in the Area of the EU's Common Security and Defence Policy," in *International Law as Law of the European Union*, ed. Enzo Cannizzaro *et al.* (Leiden: Nijhoff, 2012), 157 and Sari, "The Conclusion of International Agreements by the European Union in the Context of ESDP," *International Comparative Law Quarterly* 57 (2007), 53.

Considered as a whole, all of these elements support the idea that the conduct of national contingents placed at the disposal of Operation *Sophia* is—as a rule—attributable to the EU, rather than to the respective contributing States.[519] An analogous solution appeared to be preferable with respect to Operation *Atalanta* as well.[520] Moreover, the EU is responsible for the conduct of all of the forces placed at its disposal, including those of non-EU countries.[521] It is true that the agreements concluded with non-EU countries usually establish the responsibility of the latter in relation to claims advanced against the personnel assigned to the mission.[522] The *inter partes* effectiveness of such agreements does not preclude, however, that claims for reparations could also be advanced directly against the EU.

As a rule, moreover, the conduct of national contingents assigned to Operation *Sophia* should, in our opinion, be attributed to the EU even in the event of activities that are not directly linked to the mandate, but are carried out within the framework of reference of the European mission; this would ensure compliance with the customary obligations of the organization. This is the case, for example, with maritime SAR activities conducted by vessels assigned to Operation *Sophia* in the course of law enforcement operations at sea.[523] Moreover, the European chain of command cannot be considered 'broken' because of the need to engage in activities that are *lato sensu* 'humanitarian', usually ascribable to States,[524] but in which the EU also plays a part.[525]

However, the responsibility of a State participating in the mission cannot be ruled out where a wrongful act depends, at least in part, on a conduct directly attributable to the State. Thus, for instance, the German administrative tribunal judged Germany to bear responsibility for exposing several suspected pirates captured by a German military vessel operating within the framework of Operation *Atalanta* to the risk of being subjected to inhuman and degrading

519 See again Sari and Wessel, "International Responsibility," 137.

520 Cf. Annoni, "International," 194 and Antonio Leandro, "L'azione delle organizzazioni internazionali in materia di pirateria marittima," in *Nuove piraterie e ordinamenti giuridici interni ed internazionali. Atti del convegno tenuto a Taranto il 16 e 17 giugno 2009*, ed. Uricchio (Bari: Cacucci, 2011), 139–140.

521 See above, Part I, para. 2.

522 See, e.g., Council Decision No. 2010/199/CFSP, March 22, 2010, on the signing and conclusion of the Agreement between the EU and Montenegro on the participation of Montenegro in the EU military operation to contribute to the deterrence, prevention and repression of acts of piracy and armed robbery off the Somali coast (operation *Atalanta*), *OJEU* L 88, 1, Annex, Article 3(h), Article 2(4).

523 See above, Part II, para. 3.

524 In this respect, cf. Daniel Ghezelbash *et al.*, "Securitization," 323–325.

525 See again stenographic record No. 18, 5, 15, 25–26.

treatments in Kenyan prisons.[526] In fact, although the Court acknowledged that the transfer to the Kenyan authorities by the German forces was to be considered an act of the EU, it also recognized that the consent expressed by Germany played a decisive role in bringing about the wrongful conduct. Consequently, every act resulting in the violation of fundamental human rights needed to be analyzed in order to verify, on each specific occasion, which entities shared responsibility for the violation.[527]

A different question regards the responsibility for wrongful acts committed by the officials of one State who board vessels of a different State. The conduct of an organ of a State placed at the disposal of another State may be attributed to the latter only if the organ is acting on behalf of and exercising the authority of the government of the State to which it has been seconded.[528] The latter State will bear no responsibility where organs of a State are sent to carry out activities or functions on behalf of the former, or even in order to pursue objectives shared by both States.[529] This is the reference legal framework with regard to the conduct of 'ship riders', who normally operate under the authority of the sending State.[530] Their presence on board a vessel may sometimes be necessary to establish the jurisdiction of the sending State over the persons captured during operations at sea and for the purpose of collecting evidence according to the procedures prescribed by the legislation of that State to enable a trial to take place promptly. The same can be said with regard to Italian judicial police officers who board vessels of NGOs flying a foreign flag which engage in SAR operations in the Central Mediterranean and have adhered to the code of conduct formulated by Italy in agreements with the European Commission.[531]

526 Cf. Verwaltungsgericht Köln, Appl. No. 25 K 4280/09, judgment of November 11, 2011, www.justiz.nrw.de/nrwe/ovgs/vg_koeln/j2011/25_K_4280_09urteil20111111.html, para. 57 (last accessed April 18, 2019). For commentary see Emanuele Sommario, "Attribution of Conduct in the Framework of CSDP Missions: Reflections on a Recent Judgment by the Higher Administrative Court of Nordrhein-Westfalen," in *Protecting Human Rights in the European Union's External Relations*, ed. Sara Poli (The Hague: Cleer, 2016), 167.

527 In this regard, see also Efthymios Papastavridis, "EUNAVOR Operation *Atalanta* off Somalia: The EU in Unchartered Legal Waters?," *International and Comparative Law Quarterly* 64 (2015), 558.

528 Cf. Article 6 DARSIWA.

529 Cf. Article 47(4) of the Commentary on the DARSIWA. Regarding the customary nature of the rule coded in Article 6 DARSIWA see Pierre-Marie Dupuy, "Relation between the International Law of Responsibility and Responsibility in Municipal Law," in *The Law of International Responsibility*, eds. James Crawford, Alain Pellet and Simon Olleson (Oxford: OUP, 2010), 182.

530 Cf. Gallagher and David, *The International Law*, 313.

531 On this issue see above, Part IV, para. 2.

However, any wrongful acts committed by organs of a third State that have boarded vessels assigned to Operation *Sophia* are treated differently, as in the case, for instance, of Libyan officials trained aboard vessels assigned to the operation. Since the end of 2016, based on a Memorandum of Understanding between the forces of Operation *Sophia* and the Libyan Government of National Accord,[532] the EU has undertaken closer collaboration with the Libyan authorities. In this context, training has been provided to the Libyan Navy and Coast Guard with the aim of ensuring that they have an adequate capability in repressing wrongful conduct perpetrated in maritime areas subject to the sovereignty of the Libyan State.[533] For the purpose of attributing responsibility for any wrongful acts of Libyan officials to the EU, it is necessary in this case to establish whether the organization had effective control over the conduct in question.[534]

The case of joint operations coordinated by Frontex is different. The difficulties in human rights accountability with respect to Frontex revolve around two main aspects. First, there is disagreement as to the extent of the Agency's accountability. While Frontex may be accountable, in addition to Member States, especially under the doctrine of positive obligations arising from human rights law, its official position remains that generally only the participating Member States are accountable for human rights violations committed during joint operations.[535] Second, there is uncertainty as to the distribution of accountability among the various actors participating in Frontex joint operations.

As said previously, the joint Frontex operations *Triton* and *Themis* were established at the request of Italy; their operational plans were adopted jointly by the European Agency and the host State, in consultation with the participating Member States. Based on an analysis of the limited information available on the operational plan of both missions, it seems that the command of Member States' assets taking part in such joint operations is alternately given to the host State or the specific State sending the border guards. The Agency mostly plays a role of coordinating and assisting national efforts.[536]

532 Memorandum of Understanding between EUNAVFOR MED Operation *Sophia* and the Libyan Coast Guard relating to the training provided to the Libyan Coast Guard and Navy by EUNAVFOR MED Operation *Sophia*, Rome, August 23, 2016.

533 Council Decision No. 2016/993/CFSP, June 20, 2016, *OJEU* L 162, Article 1(1). The start-up of training activities was then authorized by the Political and Security Committee with Decision No. 2016/1635/CFSP, August 30, 2016, *OJEU* L 243, Article 1; see also stenographic record No. 18, 13–14.

534 See again Article 7 DARIO.

535 See above, Part I, para. 4.

536 See above, Part I, paras. 3 and 4.

Therefore, some legal commentators consider that the wrongful conduct of the guest officers should be considered as an act of the host State whenever the guest officer acted while exercising elements of the governmental authority of the host State;[537] however, this does not rule out a joint responsibility of the sending State for not having fulfilled the due diligence obligation to prevent any violation of human rights. Other commentators, relying on the fact that the sending State maintains some control over its officers, consider that both the host State and the sending State can be held responsible for a wrongful act committed during a joint operation on the basis of Article 17 DARSIWA. In this case, it is necessary to assess, case by case, to which entities the wrongful act is ascribable.[538]

In both cases, however, a 'shared responsibility' of the States taking part in the joint Frontex operation and the Agency can be established.[539] According to this line of reasoning, the responsibility of the EU Member States concerned, together with that of the EU, may give rise to a shared responsibility, that is, a situation where "the responsibility of two or more actors for their contribution to a particular [harmful] outcome is distributed to them separately, rather than resting on them collectively", provided that individual causal contributions cannot be determined.[540]

The possibility that the EU may incur responsibility when contributing to the implementation of Frontex joint operations is stressed by several authors[541] and this perspective seems to find validation also under Article 5 Frontex Regulation No. 2016/1624 in so far as it affirms the existence of a shared responsibility between the Agency and the Member States engaged in the joint management of the maritime borders. This situation may arise, for instance, whenever the EU, despite having the possibility of effectively influencing the conduct of the States taking part in the operation, does not adopt all the appropriate measures to prevent the violation. Another case can be seen when the Frontex Executive Director, despite having the possibility, fails to suspend or terminate, in whole or in part, a joint operation that has proved to seriously affect fundamental human rights.[542]

537 Article 6 DARSIWA.

538 Above, Part I, para. 4.

539 See again above, Part I, para. 4.

540 André Nollkaemper and Dov Jacobs, "Shared Responsibility in International Law: A Conceptual Framework," *Michigan Journal of International Law* 34 (2013): 362 and 368. For further considerations on the issue of shared responsibility see Serena Forlati, "Violazione dell'obbligo di prevenire il genocidio e riparazione nell'affare Bosnia-Erzegovina c. Serbia," *Rivista di diritto internazionale* 40 (2007): 425.

541 See, among others, Liguori and Ricciuti, "Frontex," 556; Gallagher and David, *The International Law*, 348.

542 See ICJ, *Application of the Convention*, 43.

Regulation No. 2016/1624 does not mention specific cases in which direct responsibility is ascribable to the EU for the activities carried out by Frontex, but some violations of the fundamental rights of persons rescued or intercepted at sea, such as the right to personal data protection, could be attributed exclusively to Frontex staff. The processing of personal data collected by the Agency is in fact subject to a rather strict regime.[543] In the event that a person complains of incurring harm as a result of the violation of one of these rules, the complaint should be addressed exclusively to the Agency, whose staff would bear sole responsibility since the authorities of the Member States remain totally excluded from these activities.[544] In contrast, the responsibility for human rights violations during SAR operations is attributable to the host Member State or, mostly, to the home Member State operating in the specific case. According to Article (8)(1)(f) and 14(2)(e) of Regulation No. 2016/1624, the Agency just provides technical and operational assistance to Member States and third countries in supporting SAR operations for persons in distress at sea which may take place during border surveillance operations at sea.[545]

However, the attribution of wrongful conduct to a State and/or international organization does not solve every issue related to the attribution of responsibility, especially in relation to the violation of human rights laws.

On the one hand, whenever conducts attributable to different entities under international law combine to determine a violation of the fundamental rights of persons rescued or apprehended at sea, there may be grounds for accusing such entities of complicity if both are subject to the same primary obligation[546] and it is possible to ascertain the contemporaneous presence of the subjective elements required under Articles 16 and 14, respectively, of the DARSIWA and DARIO.[547] Thus, for example, the above-mentioned role played by the

543 Cf. Articles 45–50 Regulation No. 2016/1624.

544 On this issue, cf. Martina Guidi, “La nuova guardia costiera e di frontiera europea e i vecchi problemi di tutela dei diritti umani fondamentali,” in *Migrazioni e Diritto internazionale: verso il superamento dell’emergenza?*, ed. Giuseppe Nesi (Naples: Scientifica, 2018), 377.

545 Cf. also Regulation No. 2014/656, Article 9.

546 Cf. again ICJ, *Application of the Convention*, paras. 420–424. In the literature, see generally James Crawford, *The International Law Commission’s Articles on State Responsibility: Introduction, Text, and Commentaries* (Cambridge: CUP, 2002), 149.

547 In both cases “knowledge of the circumstances of the internationally wrongful act” is required: cf. Helmut Philipp Aust, *Complicity and the Law of State Responsibility* (Cambridge: CUP, 2011) and John Quigley, “Complicity in International Law: A New Direction in the Law of State Responsibility,” *British Yearbook of International Law* 57 (1987): 57.

EU in training the Libyan Coast Guard does not appear sufficient grounds for considering the organization to be complicit in the violation of a core principle under customary law, i.e. the prohibition of *refoulement*—or other customary norms concerning fundamental human rights—in respect of naval operations conducted by the Libyan Coast Guard starting from May 2017 with the aim of intercepting vessels sailing from Libya and escorting them back to the port of origin.[548] However, the financial assistance provided by Frontex for the joint operations of the EU Member States in the Central Mediterranean and its contribution to defining the operational plan of the mission could lead to different solutions in the case of fundamental human rights violations in the context of operations *Triton* and *Themis*.

Finally, one should rightly ask if a charge of complicity may be levelled against the EU and/or Italy in the event of wrongful acts committed by the Libyan Coast Guard, given the prominent role they play in the implementation of bilateral policies agreed with Libya. Thus, for instance, some authors support the idea of Italy's international responsibility for complicity in human rights violations committed by the Libyan authorities, due to the logistical, technical and financial support provided to them.[549] However, in some cases, the level of control over the operations described, for instance, in the *Open Arms* case, appears to go far beyond mere complicity and justifies the affirmation of Italian jurisdiction under the ECHR with a direct responsibility of Italy for wrongful conducts committed by the Libyan authorities.[550] In the *Open Arms* case, a patrol boat supplied by Italy to the Libyans and operating under the coordination of the Italian Navy has carried out a repatriation clearly contrary to the principle of *non-refoulement*.[551] However, the exercise of an effective control by the Italian Navy and MRCC must be verified on a case by case basis:

548 Cf. Article 14 DARIO. For a description of the first operation conducted by the Libyan Coast Guard, see Jean-Pierre Gauci, "Back to Old Tricks? Italian Responsibility for Returning People to Libya," *EJIL: Talk!*, June 6, 2017.

549 De Vittor, "Responsabilità," 23; Giuseppe Pascale, "Is Italy Internationally Responsible for the Gross Human Rights Violations against migrants in Libya?," *Questions of International Law. Zoom-in* 56 (2019): 37.

550 De Vittor, "Soccorso," 445; Violeta Moreno-Lax and Martin Lemberg-Pedersen, "Border-Induced Displacement: The Ethical and Legal Implications of Distance-Creation through Externalization," *Questions of International Law, Zoom-in* 56 (2019): 30.

551 The intervention of the Libyan authorities was in fact the result of instructions given to the Libyans by the Italian MRCC and there was a continuous dialogue and cooperation between the Libyans and the Italian authorities throughout the operation, aimed at favoring the Libyan intervention.

Italian jurisdiction, in fact, cannot be established with respect to all operations carried out by the Libyan Coast Guard.[552]

On the other hand, as mentioned earlier, in the case of human rights laws, States have both the obligation to comply with primary legislation and the obligation to guarantee the enjoyment of those rights by all individuals within the State's jurisdiction.[553] This means, for instance, that the flag State of a vessel boarded by ship riders must monitor their conduct so as to prevent possible violations of the human rights of any individuals apprehended.

Libya also bears the obligation to prevent all human rights violations on board ships flying the Libyan flag and in every other area subject to the State's sovereignty. However, these are not obligations to achieve a specific result: the State will be considered to have fulfilled its obligations provided that it does everything in its power to prevent such violations. In the case of Libya, moreover, even if the State is not yet in a position to fully exercise its functions of control over its territory and territorial waters,[554] it cannot avoid international responsibility for human rights violations committed there or on land.[555] Thus, for instance, the State could be held responsible for the exercise of police powers in its territorial waters whenever the Libyan Coast Guard resorts to a disproportionate use of force when engaging in law enforcement operations. The same also holds true in case of ill-treatments or acts of torture perpetrated by non-State actors at Libyan detention centres.

2 *The Efficacy of Monitoring Mechanisms*

The final step of our analysis relates to the enforcement of responsibility. The aim is to find out what remedies the individual victim of a violation of his fundamental human rights in the context of naval operations in the Mediterranean Sea has at his disposal. With respect to fundamental human rights violations committed by Italy or other States individually involved in law enforcement operations at sea, domestic courts and, ultimately, the ECtHR have jurisdiction. In this respect, the analysis is mainly focused on the EU Frontex operations and on the military Operation *Sophia*.

On several occasions, Frontex has been criticized in connection with numerous incidents involving human rights violations in the context of joint

552 See again De Vittor, "Soccorso," 445.

553 See above, Part II, para. 2.

554 See above, Introduction.

555 See, *mutatis mutandis*, ECtHR, GC, *Ilaşcu et al. v Moldova and Russia*, Appl. No. 48787/99, judgment of July 8, 2004, paras. 313, 330–331 and 392.

operations. Criticisms of this sort have been voiced by some NGOs active in the protection of human rights,[556] by the European Ombudsman[557] and by the European Parliament.[558]

As the EU has not yet acceded to the ECHR, Frontex's responsibility cannot be made to bear before the Court of Strasbourg, but only before the CJEU. Since the Treaty of Lisbon entered into force, in fact, the jurisdiction of the CJEU has been extended to acts of EU agencies. Two procedures are particularly relevant to Frontex's operational activities: the action for annulment of acts of the Agency (Article 263(1) TFEU) and the failure to act procedure (Article 265(1) TFEU).[559] In addition, the Frontex Regulation alludes to the compensation for damages procedure (Article 60(3) Regulation No. 2016/1624).

Action for annulment refers to judicial review of the legality of acts intended to produce legal effects towards third parties. Among the grounds on which such review may be sought, the infringement of the Treaties or any rule of law relating to their application (Article 263(2) TFEU), which is construed to embrace violation of fundamental rights, is the most pertinent in the context of Frontex conduct. Arguably, this ground would also include a breach of the secondary legislation binding on Frontex.[560] However, there are two main obstacles to the possibility for individuals to rely on this remedy in relation to Frontex operations. On the one hand, any measure adopted by the Agency, such as the operational plan, would need to be qualified as an act producing legal effects. This means that the measure must have legal effects that are binding on the applicant and bring a change in his legal situation.[561] In this respect, an operational plan laying down mandatory instructions could be construed as an act producing legal effects. A second difficulty relates to the status of individuals as 'non-privileged applicants'. In fact, in order to be accorded standing, private applicants must be the addressees of the act, or prove that it is of 'direct

556 Cf. Daniela Vitiello, "La cooperazione operativa tra Frontex e i Paesi terzi nel contrasto all'immigrazione irregolare," in *Le migrazioni in Europa: UE, Stati terzi e migration outsourcing*, ed. Francesco Cherubini (Rome: Bordeaux, 2015), 163.

557 Cf. Letter from the European Ombudsman to the Frontex concerning his draft recommendation of April 9, 2013, case OI/5/2012/BEH-MHZ, November 12, 2013.

558 European Parliament, Resolution 2015/2660(RSP), on the latest tragedies in the Mediterranean and EU migration and asylum policies, point 1.

559 Izabella Majcher, "Human Rights Violations During EU Border Surveillance and Return Operations: Frontex's Shared Responsibility or Complicity?," *Silesian Journal of Legal Studies* 7 (2015): 70.

560 Paul Craig and Gráinne de Búrca, *EU Law: Text, Cases, and Materials* (5th edn. Oxford: OUP, 2011), 525.

561 CJEU, *IBM v Commission*, Case 60/81, judgment of November 11, 1981, para. 9.

and individual concern' to them (Article 263(4) TFEU)[562] but the operational plan would hardly meet this criteria.

The failure to act procedure offers individuals the possibility to challenge Frontex's omissions. The procedure applies to circumstances where the defendants have positive obligations under EU law to perform specific tasks; in particular, there must be a clear duty rather than a mere discretion to act.[563] The measure whose absence is challenged before the CJEU should be an act producing a legal effect. Arguably, the failure by the Agency's Director to abort a joint operation in spite of violations of human rights could be brought within the scope of this remedy (Article 25(4) Regulation No. 2016/1624). In fact, the Frontex Regulation provides for an obligation incumbent on the head of the Agency to terminate or suspend the mission if it violates fundamental rights. Presumably, an act terminating an operation would have binding legal force and leave no discretion to the host State. In this case as well, the individual petitioners would need to prove that the measure that Frontex failed to adopt was of 'direct and individual concern' to them (Article 265(3) TFEU).

Finally, pursuant to the Frontex Regulation (Article 60(3)), the Agency should assume its non-contractual responsibility before the CJEU in all disputes concerning damage caused by the Agency's staff. Under this procedure, the Court decides on claims of damage caused by EU institutions or its servants—including Frontex staff—in the performance of their duties (Articles 268 and 340(2) TFEU). However, unlike under the regime of international responsibility, under EU law not every wrongful act triggers responsibility. In particular, the rule allegedly infringed must confer rights on individuals and the breach should have a manifest and grave character.[564] The second condition recognizes the margin of appreciation enjoyed by the perpetrator. Accordingly, the broader Frontex's staff discretionary power is, the higher the threshold required to consider their breaches sufficiently serious.[565] Finally,

562 'Direct concern' is established when the measure directly affects the legal situation of the applicant and leaves no discretion to national authorities as to its implementation (CJEU, GC, *National Front v European Parliament*, Case C-468/01 P, judgment of June 29, 2004, para. 34). To prove individual concern, the applicants need to show that they have attributes or characteristics distinguishing them from all other persons and mark them out in the same manner as the addressees of the measure (CJEU, *Plaumann et al. v Commission*, Case 25/62, judgment of July 15, 1963).

563 Majcher, "Human Rights," 71.

564 CJEU, *Laboratoires Pharmaceutiques Bergaderm SA and Jean-Jacques Goupil v Commission*, Case C-352/98 P, judgment of July 4, 2000, para. 42.

565 Jean-Marc Thouvenin, "Responsibility in the Context of the European Union Legal Order," in *The Law of International Responsibility*, eds. James Crawford, Alain Pellet and Simon Olleson (Oxford: OUP, 2010), 868–871.

Frontex's accountability requires the plaintiff to demonstrate a causal link between the Agency's conduct and the damage caused. In some cases a causal link seems to be easily established, for example in cases where the Executive Director fails to suspend or terminate an operation seriously damaging fundamental human rights.[566]

As seen, however, legal remedies against an international organization's acts are difficult to implement and enforce in practice. Thus, non-judicial scrutiny by some monitoring mechanisms internal to the Agency has been perceived as a way to fill in the accountability gap. Among them, the Consultative Forum on Fundamental Rights, established in October 2012, has the function of advising and assisting the Frontex Director and the Management Board in fundamental rights matters by providing them with independent consultation.[567] A key role in this respect is assigned to the Fundamental Rights Officer, created in September 2012; the introduction of this figure has undoubtedly fostered administrative scrutiny over the Agency's actions. Designated by the Management Board and appointed by the Director, the Fundamental Rights Officer reports directly to the Director, the Board, and the Consultative Forum and contributes to monitoring the mechanism of fundamental rights by regularly reporting on Frontex's activities and drawing up and maintaining a record of possible fundamental rights incidents that may occur during Frontex operations. Since 2016 the Fundamental Rights Officer has also been responsible for handling complaints from individuals.[568] The Agency has thus finally implemented the recommendation, adopted by the European Ombudsman in the framework of the inquiry undertaken on her own initiative in 2012, to provide for an internal complaint mechanism.[569] However, the mechanism still shows some opacity in its implementation and does not seem to be fully independent and effective.[570]

Traditionally, national courts refuse to adjudicate complaints against international organizations because of the immunity of jurisdiction they enjoy in their Member States.[571] Frontex is no different in this respect: in fact, the

566 On this issue, see also Liguori and Ricciuti, "Frontex," 565.

567 Cf. Article 70 Regulation No. 2016/1624.

568 Cf. Article 72 Regulation No. 2016/1624.

569 European Ombudsman, "Special Report of the European Ombudsman in Own-Initiative Inquiry OI/5/2012/BEH-MHZ Concerning Frontex," November 7, 2013; cf. also Majcher, "Human Rights," 75.

570 Cf. also Guidi, "La nuova," 394.

571 The underlying rationale for granting immunities to international organizations is to ensure their independence from States and their effective functioning: see Jan Klabbers, *An Introduction to International Institutional Law* (3rd edn. Cambridge: CUP, 2015), 131–152.

Agency enjoys such privileges and immunities in the EU States as are necessary for the performance of its tasks.[572] However, the immunity from legal process may encroach upon the right of access to a court, as set out in Article 6 ECHR and Article 47 CFREU. In this regard, the ECtHR has ruled that granting jurisdictional immunity to international organizations would be permissible under the ECHR, as long as the applicants have access to reasonable alternative remedies, including internal review mechanisms.[573]

The Court's reasoning implies that, in the absence of an adequate alternative review mechanism available to the petitioner, domestic courts should waive the immunities. At present, there are hardly any accessible alternative appeal mechanisms available to individuals affected by Frontex's operations. Redress is difficult to obtain through the CJEU due to legal impediments to individuals, while the Court's recent negative opinion on EU accession to the ECHR precludes the ECtHR's scrutiny of Frontex's conduct in the near future. Thus, only if the violations of the fundamental human rights complained of are ascribable to operations of the border guards conducted under the command and control of a Member State, and are consequently attributable to it, can individuals turn to the Court of Strasbourg, after having exhausted all domestic jurisdictional remedies.

It is true that the Agency has developed significant tools to strengthen fundamental rights protection in its activities. However, several observers and institutional actors remain concerned about whether these changes alone may effectively address all the human rights issues at stake. In fact, even if the Agency finally established a quasi-judicial internal claims mechanism, as noted earlier, it currently does not seem to be fully transparent and effective. As a consequence, if an individual files a complaint against Frontex before a court in one of the EU Member States, the Agency's immunity may need to be waived. Otherwise the claimant's right of access to justice risks being violated.[574]

On the other hand, any human rights violations committed in the context of Operation *Sophia* will have to be examined before national courts and, where necessary, before the ECtHR, in light of the case-law that has been built up

572 Article 18 Protocol on the Privileges and Immunities of the European Communities.

573 Cf. ECtHR, *Beer and Regan v Germany*, Appl. No. 28934/95, judgment of February 18, 1999, para. 58; ECtHR, *Waite and Kennedy v Germany*, Appl. No. 26083/94, judgment of February 18, 1999, para. 68. For a commentary see Cedric Ryngaert, "The Immunity of International Organizations before Domestic Courts: Recent Trends," *International Organizations Law Review* 7 (2010): 132–144.

574 Majcher, "Human Rights," 73–74.

starting from the *Bosphorus* case.[575] In truth, whenever States Parties to the Convention transfer sovereign powers to an international organization, they remain responsible for the conduct of their organs "regardless of whether the act or omission was a consequence of domestic law or of the necessity to comply with international legal obligations."[576] It is well known that the CJEU does not have jurisdiction over the activities carried out within the framework of the CSDP;[577] however, in these cases the EU does not enjoy immunity before the courts of its Member States.[578]

3 *Concluding Remarks*

The above analysis shows that the naval operations aimed at tackling human trafficking and migrant smuggling across the Central Mediterranean Sea give rise to a range of issues as regards the respect for the fundamental human rights of the individuals involved, whether they are migrants, smugglers and traffickers or third parties not involved in unlawful activities at sea.

The EU multinational operations in the Mediterranean have shown to be effective in the capture of people smugglers; however, a more intense effort is required on the part of the international community if the objective of disrupting the transnational network engaged in such unlawful activities is to be met. More significant results could be achieved by extending the theatre of activity of Operation *Sophia* to areas subject to the sovereignty of Libya. In fact, one of the largest problems to emerge in the course of this operation consists precisely in the lack of a transition from the stage of operations conducted on the high seas to one in Libya's own territorial waters, inland waters and territory. The objective has not been achieved due to the reluctance of the Libyan authorities to provide the necessary consent, and also because of the opposition of Russia and China within the UN Security Council.[579] Furthermore, notwithstanding Operation *Sophia*'s mandate was recently extended until September 30, 2019, it does no longer involve maritime presence in the Mediterranean. The decision of ending the deployment of ships and limiting its means to the air assets

575 Cf. ECtHR, *Bosphorus Hava Yollari Turizm ve ticaret anonim Sirketi v Ireland*, Appl. No. 45036/98, judgment of June 30, 2005.

576 Ibid., para. 153. For an analysis of the judgment, see Tobias Lock, "Beyond *Bosphorus*: The European Court of Human Rights' Case Law on the Responsibility of Member States of International Organisations under the European Convention on Human Rights," *Human Rights Law Review* 10 (2010): 529.

577 Cf. Articles 24(1) TEU and 275(2) TFEU and Naert, "The International Responsibility," 331.

578 Cf. Articles 274 TFEU and 19(1) TFEU, as well as Naert, "The International Responsibility," 331.

579 In this regard, see Gestri, "EUNAVFOR MED," 36.

only was largely due to the growing hostility towards the operation. The new Italian Government, in fact, had threatened to veto the renewal of the mission's mandate for as long as disembarkation of persons by the ships operating under its auspices was to take place only in Italy.

It emerges clearly that the multinational operations in the Mediterranean may result in multiple violations of both customary and treaty obligations established under the international law of the sea, as well as obligations established for the protection of human rights. More precisely, the regime of responsibility that has developed in the context of Operation *Sophia* tends to assign an exclusive responsibility to the EU for the wrongful acts committed by the assets placed at the organization's disposal by States taking part in the operation, unless the organization loses control over the 'seconded' contingents. However, a regime of joint responsibility between the EU and an individual contributing State may arise whenever a wrongful act is due, at least in part, to conduct directly attributable to that State.[580] As regards Frontex operations, a shared responsibility of the States taking part in the joint operations and the Agency can be established most of the time, even if only a case-by-case assessment can define to which entities the wrongful act is ascribable in each individual single case. However, in some cases, the Agency or a State taking part in the operation may also be found to bear exclusive responsibility for some wrongful conducts. The monitoring mechanisms currently provided by both EU Law and in the context of the Council of Europe cannot be considered as fully effective when it comes to sanctioning violations of individual human rights committed in the context of these naval operations.

Finally, the strengthening of the operational capacities of the Libyan authorities in patrolling the areas subject to the sovereignty of Libya and the prominent role entrusted to Italy raise further doubts as to the latest developments of operations in the area. Italian cooperation with the Libyan authorities is problematic mainly as regards compliance with fundamental human rights obligations binding for Italy, and in particular the *non-refoulement* obligation. Given the persisting inhuman conditions of detention given to migrants and the continued absence of an effective system for receiving asylum seekers in Libya, the State cannot be considered a 'safe place' for the disembarkation of migrants. Italian and EU support of the Libyan Coast Guard is explained to some degree by the need to strengthen and stabilize the central power and is aimed at achieving a positive effect on the migratory flow. However, until it is not proven that the situation in Libya is such as to ensure the reception of migrants while respecting their fundamental rights, it will not be possible

580 See above, Part 1, para. 4.

for migrants to be sent back to Libya.[581] Different instructions possibly given by the competent MRCC represent an abuse of right: the Libyan SRR was in fact established arbitrarily since a safe harbor cannot be currently found in that State. Furthermore, such acts are ascribable to Italy by way of complicity with respect to wrongful conducts committed by Libyan authorities and a direct responsibility of Italy can also be established whenever the Italian Navy and MRCC are shown to exercise an effective control over the operations performed by the Libyan vessels. Moreover, the European Parliament and the Commissioner for human rights of the Council of Europe have expressed their wish for concrete actions aimed at consolidating the Libyan State by making cooperation with the Libyan Coast Guard subordinate to the establishment of precise procedures for monitoring the respect of the fundamental rights of migrants.[582]

The analysis of the situation developed from a human rights perspective shows that there is the need for a full reconsideration of current policies implemented by international actors in that maritime area in order to tackle the illegal trafficking of persons. First, the opening of channels for safe and legal arrival into Europe is needed, together with a legal reform of EU national legislations criminalizing SAR activities at sea when performed by private actors. In this respect, an important burden-sharing element may help Member States positioned at the external borders of the EU, like Italy, to cope with disembarkations is a flexible list of safe harbours along the European coastline willing to accept disembarkations of migrants rescued at sea.

Acknowledgements

This work takes into account the law as it stood, to the best of the author's knowledge, on July 4, 2019. This book would not have been possible without the funding of the University of Macerata—Department of Political Science, Communication and International Relations. I gratefully acknowledge its contribution.

581 De Vittor, "Soccorso," 450.

582 European Parliament, Recommendation to the Council, the Commission, and the EEAS on Libya, May 30, 2018, 2018/2017(INI), http://www.europarl.europa.eu (last accessed April 18, 2019); CoE, Commissioner for human rights, "Lives Saved. Rights Protected. Bridging the Protection Gap for Refugees and Migrants in the Mediterranean," June 2019, available at: https://www.coe.int (last accessed on June 26, 2019), 43–44.

Bibliography

Allain, Jean, "The *Jus Cogens* Nature of *Non-Refoulement*," *International Journal of Refugee Law* 13 (2001): 533–558.

Amalfitano, Chiara, *Conflitti di giurisdizione e riconoscimento delle decisioni penali nell'Unione europea* (Milan: Giuffrè, 2006).

Annoni, Alessandra, "L'esercizio dell'azione penale nei confronti dei trafficanti di migranti: le responsabilità dell'Italia … e quelle degli altri," *SIDI Blog*, May 6, 2015.

Annoni, Alessandra, "International Action against Piracy and Armed Robbery at Sea off the Coast of Somalia," *Italian Yearbook of International Law* 23 (2013): 175–198.

Annoni, Alessandra, "Il ruolo delle operazioni *Triton* e *Sophia* nella repressione della tratta di esseri umani e del traffico di migranti nel Mediterraneo centrale," *Il diritto dell'Unione Europea* 4 (2017): 829–859.

Annoni, Alessandra, "Traffico di migranti via mare: l'ambito di applicazione della legge penale italiana," *Rivista di diritto della navigazione* 44 (2015): 420–432.

Anrò, Ilaria, *L'adesione dell'Unione Europea alla CEDU. L'evoluzione dei sistemi di tutela dei diritti fondamentali in Europa* (Milan: Giuffrè, 2015).

Aust, Helmut Philipp, *Complicity and the Law of State Responsibility* (Cambridge: CUP, 2011).

Baillet, Cecilia, "The *Tampa Case* and Its Impact on Burden Sharing at Sea," *Human Rights Quarterly* 25 (2003): 741–774.

Baratta, Roberto, "Le principali novità del Trattato di Lisbona," *Diritto dell'Unione Europea* 13 (2008): 21–70.

Barnes, Richard, "The International Law of the Sea and Migration Control," in *Extraterritorial Immigration Control: Legal Challenges*, eds. Bernard Ryan and Valsamis Mitsilegas (Leiden: Nijhoff, 2010), 103–149.

Barnes, Richard, "Refugee Law at Sea," *International and Comparative Law Quarterly* 53 (2004): 47–77.

Bartolini, Giulio, "Attribution of Conduct and Liability Issues Arising from International Disaster Relief Missions," *Vanderbilt Journal of Transnational Law* 48 (2015), 1029–1058.

Baumgärtel, Moritz, "High Risk, High Reward: Taking the Question of Italy's Involvement in Libyan 'Pullback' Policies to the European Court of Human Rights," *EJIL: Talk!*, May 14, 2018.

Bevilacqua, Giorgia, "Exploring the Ambiguity of Operation Sophia between Military and Search and Rescue Activities," in *The Future of the Law of the Sea. Bridging Gaps between National, Individual and Common Interests*, ed. Gemma Andreone (Heidelberg: Springer, 2017), 165–179.

Bevilacqua, Giorgia, *Criminalità e sicurezza in alto mare* (Naples: Scientifica, 2017).

Bo, Marta, "Repressing Migrant Smuggling by the UN Security Council and EU Naval Military Operation Sophia: Some Reflections on Jurisdiction and Human Rights," *EJIL: Talk!*, November 3, 2017.

Bruin, Rene and Wouters, Kees, "Terrorism and the Non-Derogability of *Non-Refoulement*," *International Journal of Refugee Law* 15 (2003): 5–29.

Butler, Graham and Ratcovich, Martin, "Operation Sophia in Uncharted Waters: European and International Law Challenges for the EU Naval Mission in the Mediterranean Sea," *Nordic Journal of International Law* 85 (2016): 235–259.

Caligiuri, Andrea, "La coopération régionale à l'épreuve de la répression pénale de la piraterie maritime," in *Stratégie logistique et de transport au service du développement en Afrique*, eds. Achaa Abdillahi Ahmed, Ibrahim Chitou and Bernadette Smeesters (Paris: L'Harmattan, 2015), 109–133.

Caligiuri, Andrea, *L'obbligo* aut dedere aut judicare *nel diritto internazionale* (Milan: Giuffrè, 2012).

Cameron, Iain, *The Protective Principle of International Criminal Jurisdiction* (Aldershot: Dartmouth, 1994).

Casolari, Federico, "The EU's Hotspot Approach to Managing the Migration Crisis: A Blind Spot for Internationally Responsibility?," *Italian Yearbook of International Law* 25 (2015): 109–134.

Cassoni, Giuseppe, *L'Organizzazione del Trattato dell'Atlantico del Nord* (Milan: Giuffrè, 1967).

Cataldi, Giuseppe, "Giurisdizione e intervento in alto mare su navi impegnate nel traffico di migranti," *Giurisprudenza Italiana* (2015): 1498–1502.

Churcill, Robin Rolf and Lowe, Alan Vaughan, *The Law of the Sea* (3rd edn. Manchester: Juris, 1999).

Cocco, Giovanni, "Dal pirata *hostis humani generis* alla pirateria contemporanea. Verso un diritto penale universale?," *Rivista italiana di diritto e procedura penale* 2 (2012): 409–463.

Condorelli, Luigi, "Le statut des forces de l'ONU et le droit international humanitaire," *Rivista di diritto internazionale* 78 (1995): 881–906.

Coppens, Jasmine, "Interception of Migrant Boats at Sea," in *'Boat Refugees' and Migrants at Sea: A Comprehensive Approach. Integrating Maritime Security with Human Rights*, eds. Violeta Moreno-Lax and Efthymios Papastavridis (Leiden: Nijhoff, 2017), 199–220.

Cottone, Marco, "Alcune notazioni in materia di reati connessi all'immigrazione clandestina via mare," in *L'immigrazione irregolare via mare nella giurisprudenza italiana e nell'esperienza europea*, eds. Amedeo Antonucci, Irini Papanicolopulu and Tullio Scovazzi (Turin: Giappichelli, 2016).

Craig, Paul and de Búrca, Gráinne, *EU Law: Text, Cases, and Materials* (5th edn. Oxford: OUP, 2011).

Crawford, James, *The International Law Commission's Articles on State Responsibility: Introduction, Text, and Commentaries* (Cambridge: CUP, 2002).

Cusumano, Eugenio, "Emptying the Sea with a Spoon? Non-Governmental Providers of Migrants Search and Rescue in the Mediterranean," *Marine Policy* 75 (2017): 91–98.

Cusumano, Eugenio, "Straightjacketing Migrant Rescuers? The Code of Conduct on Maritime NGOs," *Mediterranean Politics* 24 (2017): 106–114.

Davies, Martin, "Obligations and Implications for Ships Encountering Persons in Need of Assistance at Sea," *Pacific Rim Law and Policy Journal* 12 (2003): 109–141.

Dean, Fabio, *Norma penale e territorio. Gli elementi di territorialità in relazione alla struttura del reato* (Milan: Giuffrè, 1963).

De Bruycker, Philippe, "The European Border and Coast Guard: A New Model Built on an Old Logic," *European Papers* 1 (2016): 559–569.

De Guttry, Andrea, *Lo status della nave da Guerra in tempo di pace* (Milan: Giuffrè, 1994).

De Sena, Pasquale and De Vittor, Francesca, "La 'minaccia' italiana di 'bloccare' gli sbarchi di migranti e il diritto internazionale," *SIDI Blog*, July 1, 2017.

De Sena, Pasquale, *La nozione di giurisdizione statale nei trattati sui diritti dell'uomo* (Turin: Giappichelli, 2002).

De Vittor, Francesca, "Responsabilità degli Stati e dell'Unione europea nella conclusione e nell'esecuzione di accordi per il controllo extraterritoriale della migrazione," *Diritti umani e diritto internazionale* 12 (2018), 5–27.

De Vittor, Francesca, "Soccorso in mare e favoreggiamento dell'immigrazione irregolare: sequestro e dissequestro della nave Open Arms," *Diritti umani e diritto internazionale* 12 (2018), 443–453.

De Vittor, Francesca, "Soccorso in mare e rimpatri in Libia: tra diritto del mare e tutela internazionale dei diritti dell'uomo," *Rivista di diritto internazionale* 92 (2009): 800–807.

Di Filippo, Marcello, "Irregular Migration and Safeguard of Life at Sea," in *International Law of the Sea: Current Trends and Controversial Issues*, ed. Angela Del Vecchio (The Hague: Eleven Internat, 2014), 9–27.

Dorigo, Stefano, "Imputazione e responsabilità internazionale per l'attività delle forze di peace-keeping delle Nazioni Unite," *Rivista di diritto internazionale* 85 (2002): 903–945.

Dupuy, Pierre-Marie, "Relation between the International Law of Responsibility and Responsibility in Municipal Law," in *The Law of International Responsibility*, eds. James Crawford, Alain Pellet and Simon Olleson (Oxford: OUP, 2010), 173–185.

Durieux, Jean-François and McAdam, Jane, "*Non-Refoulement* through Time. The Case for a Derogation Clause to the Refugee Convention in Mass Influx Emergencies," *International Journal of Refugee Law* 16 (2004): 4–24.

Favilli, Chiara, "La cooperazione UE-Turchia per contenere il flusso dei migranti e richiedenti asilo: obiettivo riuscito?," *Diritti umani e diritto internazionale* 10 (2016): 405–426.

Favilli, Chiara, "Quali modalità di conclusione degli accordi internazionali in materia di immigrazione," *Rivista di diritto internazionale* 88 (2005): 156–165.

Ferri, Federico, "Il Codice di condotta per le ONG e i diritti dei migranti: fra diritto internazionale e politiche europee," *Diritti umani e diritto internazionale* 12 (2018): 189–198.

Fiengo, Gaspare, "Brevi note sulle 'missioni' dell'Unione europea per la gestione di crisi internazionali," *Il diritto dell'Unione Europea* (2016): 551–570.

Fink, Melanie, *Frontex and Human Rights: Responsibility in 'Multi-Actor Situations' under the ECHR and EU Public Liability Law* (Oxford: OUP, 2018).

Fink, Melanie and Gombeer, Kristof, "The Aquarius Incident: Navigating the Turbulent Waters of International Law," *EJIL: Talk!*, June 14, 2018.

Fink, Melanie, "Salami Slicing Human Rights Accountability: How the European Border and Coast Guard Agency may Inherit Frontex' Genetic Defect," *EJIL: Talk!*, March 10, 2016.

Fink, Melanie, "Frontex Working Arrangements: Legitimacy and Human Rights Concerns Regarding 'Technical Relationships'," *Merkourios* 28 (2012): 20–35.

Forlati, Serena, "Violazione dell'obbligo di prevenire il genocidio e riparazione nell'affare Bosnia-Erzegovina c. Serbia," *Rivista di diritto internazionale* 40 (2007): 425–430.

Francioni, Francesco, "Maritime Terrorism and International Law: The Rome Convention of 1988," *German Yearbook of International Law* 31 (1988): 263–287.

Frulli, Micaela, *Le operazioni di peacekeeping delle Nazioni Unite: continuità di un modello normativo* (Naples: Scientifica, 2012).

Gaja, Giorgio, "The Co-Respondent Mechanism According to the Draft Agreement for the Accession of the EU to the ECHR," *ESIL Reflections*, January 9, 2013.

Gaja, Giorgio, "The Relations between the European Union and Its States from the Perspective of the ILC Articles on Responsibility of International Organizations," *SHARES Research Paper* 25 (2013).

Gaja, Giorgio, "Responsabilité des Etats et/ou des organisations internationales en cas de violations des droits de l'homme," in *La soumission des organisations internationales aux normes internationales relatives aux droits de l'homme* (Paris: Pedone, 2009), 17–25.

Gallagher, Anne and David, Fiona, *The International Law of Migrant Smuggling* (Cambridge: CUP, 2014).

García Andrade, Paula, "Extraterritorial Strategies to Tackle Irregular Migration by Sea," in *Extraterritorial Immigration Control: Legal Challenges*, eds. Bernard Ryan and Valsamis Mitsilegas (Leiden: Nijhoff, 2010), 311–345.

Gauci, Jean-Pierre, "Back to Old Tricks? Italian Responsibility for Returning People to Libya," *EJIL: Talk!*, June 6, 2017.

Gautier, Philippe, "The Reparation for Injuries Case Revisited: The Personality of the European Union," *Max Plank Yearbook of United Nations Law* 4 (2000): 331–361.

Gazzini, Tarcisio, "NATO's Role in the Collective Security System," *Journal of Conflict and Security Law* 8 (2003): 231–263.

Geiβ, Robin and Petrig, Anna, *Piracy and Armed Robbery at Sea. The Legal Framework for Counter-Piracy Operations in Somalia and the Gulf of Aden* (Oxford: OUP, 2011).

Gestri, Marco, "EUNAVFOR MED: Fighting Migrant Smuggling under UN Security Council Resolution 2240 (2015)," *Italian Yearbook of International Law* 25 (2016): 21–54.

Gestri, Marco, "La politica europea dell'immigrazione: solidarietà tra Stati membri e misure nazionali di regolarizzazione," in *Problemi e tendenze del diritto internazionale dell'economia. Liber amicorum in onore di Paolo Picone*, eds. Aldo Ligustro and Giorgio Sacerdoti (Naples: Scientifica, 2011), 895–925.

Ghezelbash, Daniel, Moreno-Lax, Violeta, Klein, Natalie and Opeskin, Brian, "Securitization of Search and Rescue at Sea: The Response to Boat Migration in the Mediterranean and Offshore Australia," *International Comparative Law Quarterly* 67 (2018): 315–351.

Giuffrè, Mariagiulia, "State Responsibility beyond Borders: What Legal Basis for Italy's Push-Backs to Libya?," *International Journal of Refugee Law* 24 (2012): 692–734.

Giuffrè, Mariagiulia, "Watered-Down Rights on the High Seas: *Hirsi Jamaa and Others v Italy*," *International and Comparative Law Quarterly* 61 (2012): 728–750.

Goodwin-Gill, Guy and McAdam, Jane, *The Refugee in International Law* (3rd edn. Oxford: OUP, 2007).

Gombeer, Kristof and Fink, Melanie, "Non-Governmental Organisations and Search and Rescue at Sea," *Maritime Safety and Security Law Journal* (2018): 1–25.

Guidi, Martina, "La nuova guardia costiera e di frontiera europea e i vecchi problemi di tutela dei diritti umani fondamentali," in *Migrazioni e Diritto internazionale: verso il superamento dell'emergenza?*, ed. Giuseppe Nesi (Naples: Scientifica, 2018), 377–401.

Guilfoyle, Douglas, "ECHR Rights at Sea: *Medvedyev and Others v. France*," *EJIL: Talk!*, April 19, 2010.

Guilfoyle, Douglas, "*Medvedyev and Others v. France*, European Court of Human Rights," *International Journal of Marine and Coastal Law* 25 (2010): 437–442.

Guilfoyle, Douglas, *Shipping Interdiction and the Law of the Sea* (Cambridge: CUP, 2009).

Heijer, Maarten den, "Europe beyond its Borders: Refugee and Human Rights Protection in Extraterritorial Immigration Control," in *Extraterritorial Immigration Control. Legal Challenges*, eds. Bernard Ryan and Valsamis Mitsilegas (Leiden: Nijhoff, 2010), 169–197.

Irrera, Daniela, "Migrants, the EU and NGOs: The 'Practice' of Non-Governmental SAR Operations," *Romanian Journal of European Affairs* 16 (2016), 20–35.

Karim, Saiful, "Is There an International Obligation to Prosecute Pirates?," *Netherlands International Law Review* 58 (2011): 387–407.

Klabbers, Jan, *An Introduction to International Institutional Law* (3rd edn. Cambridge: CUP, 2015).

Klug, Anja and Howe, Tim, "The Concept of State Jurisdiction and the Applicability of the *Non-Refoulement* Principle to Extraterritorial Interception Measures," in *Extraterritorial Immigration Control. Legal Challenges*, eds. Bernard Ryan and Valsamis Mitsilegas (Leiden: Nijhoff, 2010), 69–101.

Kneebone, Susan, McDowell, Christopher and Morrell, Gareth, "A Mediterranean Solution? Chances of Success," *International Journal of Refugee Law* 18 (2006): 492–508.

Komp, Lisa-Marie, "The Duty to Assist Persons in Distress: An Alternative Source of Protection against the Return of Migrants and Asylum Seekers to the High Seas?," in *'Boat Refugees' and Migrants at Sea: A Comprehensive Approach*, eds. Violeta Moreno-Lax and Efthymios Papastavridis (Leiden: Nijhoff, 2016), 222–247.

Koutrakos, Panos, "International Agreements in the Area of the EU's Common Security and Defence Policy," in *International Law as Law of the European Union*, eds. Enzo Cannizzaro, Paolo Palchetti and Ramses Wessel (Leiden: Nijhoff, 2012), 157–187.

Koutrakos, Panos, *The EU Common Security and Defence Policy* (Oxford: OUP, 2013).

Kuijper, Pieter Jan, *The Law of EU External Relations: Cases, Materials and Commentary on the EU as an International Actor* (2nd edn. Oxford: OUP, 2015).

Kuijper, Pieter Jan and Paasivirta, Esa, "EU International Responsibility and Its Attribution: From the Inside Looking Out," in *The International Responsibility of the European Union: European and International Perspectives*, eds. Malcolm Evans and Panos Koutrakos (Oxford: Hart, 2013), 35–73.

Kuijper, Pieter Jan and Paasivirta, Esa, "Does One Size Fit All? The European Community and the Responsibility of International Organizations," *Netherlands Yearbook of International Law* 36 (2005): 169–226.

Lauterpacht, Elihu and Bethlehem, Daniel, "The Scope and Content of the Principle of *Non-Refoulement*," in *Refugee Protection in International Law*, eds. Erika Feller, Volker Türk and Frances Nicholson (Cambridge: CUP, 2003), 87–177.

Leandro, Antonio, "L'azione delle organizzazioni internazionali in materia di pirateria marittima," in *Nuove piraterie e ordinamenti giuridici interni ed internazionali. Atti del convegno tenuto a Taranto il 16 e 17 giugno 2009*, ed. Antonio Uricchio (Bari: Cacucci, 2011), 121–140.

Leanza, Umberto and Graziani, Francesca, "Poteri di *enforcement* e di *jurisdiction* in materia di traffico di migranti via mare: aspetti operativi nell'attività di contrasto," *La Comunità internazionale* 69 (2014): 163–209.

Leck, Christopher, "International Responsibility in United Nations Peacekeeping Operations: Command and Control Arrangements and the Attribution of Conduct," *Melbourne Journal of International Law* 10 (2009): 346–364.

Lehmann, Julian, "Rights at the Frontier: Border Control and Human Rights Protection of Irregular International Migrants," *Goettingen Journal of International Law* 3 (2011): 733–775.

Liguori, Anna, *Migration Law and the Externalization of Border Controls. European State Responsibility* (London: Routledge, 2019).

Liguori, Anna and Ricciuti, Novella, "Frontex ed il rispetto dei diritti umani nelle operazioni congiunte alle frontiere esterne dell'Unione europea," *Diritti umani e diritto internazionale* 6 (2012): 539–567.

Lock, Tobias, "Beyond *Bosphorus*: The European Court of Human Rights' Case Law on the Responsibility of Member States of International Organisations under the European Convention on Human Rights," *Human Rights Law Review* 10 (2010): 529–545.

Lowe, Alan, "The Right of Entry into Maritime Ports in International Law," *San Diego Law Review* 14 (1977): 597–622.

Magi, Laura, "Criminal Conduct on the High Seas: Is a General Rule on Jurisdiction Still Missing?," *Rivista di diritto internazionale* 98 (2015): 79–113.

Magi, Laura, "Protezione dei richiedenti asilo 'par ricochet' o protezione 'par moitié'?, La Grande Camera ripatisce fra gli Stati contraenti le responsabilità per violazioni della Convenzione europea conseguenti al trasferimento di un richiedente asilo in attuazione del regolamento Dublino II," *Rivista di diritto internazionale* 94 (2011): 824–832.

Majcher, Izabella, "Human Rights Violations During EU Border Surveillance and Return Operations: Frontex's Shared Responsibility or Complicity?," *Silesian Journal of Legal Studies* 7 (2015): 45–78.

Mallia, Patricia, *Migrant Smuggling by Sea. Combating a Current Threat to Maritime Security through the Creation of a Cooperative Framework* (Leiden: Nijhoff, 2010).

Mancini, Marina, "Italy's New Migration Control Policy: Stemming the Flow of Migrants from Libya without Regard for Their Human Rights," *Italian Yearbook of International Law* 27 (2017): 259–281.

Mann, Frederick Alexander, "The Doctrine of Jurisdiction in International Law," *Recueil des cours* (1964): 1–162.

Markard, Nora, "The Right to Leave by Sea: Legal Limits on EU Migration Control by Third Countries," *European Journal of International Law* 27 (2016): 591–616.

Mastrojeni, Marcello, "I limiti spaziali di applicazione della legge penale e i rapporti con giurisdizioni straniere," in *La legge, penale, il reato, il reo, la persona offesa*, ed. Giancarlo De Vero (Turin: Giappichelli, 2010), 99–105.

Marx, Reinhard, "*Non-Refoulement*, Access to Procedures and Responsibility for Determining Refugee Claims," *International Journal of Refugee Law* 7 (1995): 383–406.

McAdam, Jane, *Complementary Protection in Refugee Law* (Oxford: OUP, 2005).

Messineo, Francesco, "Things Could Only Get Better: *Al-Jedda* Beyond *Behrami*," *Military Law and the Law of War Review* 50 (2011): 321–346.

Moreno-Lax, Violeta and Giuffré, Mariagiulia, "The Raise of Consensual Containment: From 'Contactless Control' to 'Contactless Responsibility' for Forced Migration Flows," in *Research Handbook on International Refugee Law*, ed. Satvinder Singh Juss (London: Edward Elgar, 2019).

Moreno-Lax, Violeta and Lemberg-Pedersen, Martin, "Border-Induced Displacement: The Ethical and Legal Implications of Distance-Creation through Externalization," *Questions of International Law, Zoom-in* 56 (2019): 5–33.

Moreno-Lax, Violeta and Costello, Cathryn, "The Extraterritorial Application of the EU Charter of Fundamental Rights: From Territoriality to Facticity. The Effectiveness Model," in *The EU Charter of Fundamental Rights: A Commentary*, eds. Steve Peers, Tamara Hervey, Jeff Kenner and Angela Ward (Oxford: Hart, 2014), 1657–1683.

Moreno-Lax, Violeta, "Seeking Asylum in the Mediterranean: Against a Fragmentary Reading of EU Member States' Obligations Accruing at Sea," *International Journal of Refugee Law* 23 (2011): 174–220.

Mungianu, Roberta, *Frontex and* Non-Refoulement*: The International Responsibility of the EU* (Cambridge: CUP, 2016).

Mungianu, Roberta, "Frontex: Towards a Common Policy on External Border Control," *European Journal of Migration and Law* 15 (2013): 359–385.

Mussi, Francesca, "The Italian Job: Human Rights Considerations of the Diciotti Incident," *Rights!*, October 18, 2018.

Naert, Frederik, "The International Responsibility of the Union in the Context of its CSDP Operations," in *The International Responsibility of the European Union. European and International Perspectives*, ed. Malcolm Evans (Oxford: Hart, 2013), 313–337.

Naert, Frederik, "The Application of International Humanitarian Law and Human Rights in CSDP Operations," in *International Law as the Law of European Union*, eds. Enzo Cannizzaro, Paolo Palchetti and Ramses Wessel (Leiden: Nijhoff, 2012), 189–212.

Naert, Frederik, *International Law Aspects of the EU's Security and Defence Policy, with a Particular Focus on the Law of Armed Conflict* (Antwerp: Intersentia, 2010).

Nollkaemper, André and Jacobs, Dov, "Shared Responsibility in International Law: A Conceptual Framework," *Michigan Journal of International Law* 34 (2013): 359–438.

O'Keefe, Roger, "Universal Jurisdiction: Clarifying the Basic Concept," *Journal of International Criminal Justice* 2 (2004): 735–760.

Palchetti, Paolo, "International Responsibility for Conduct of UN Peacekeeping Forces: The Question of Attribution," in *Refining Human Rights Obligations in Conflict Situations*, ed. Paolo Palchetti (The Hague: Asser Press, 2014), 1–29.

Papanicolopulu, Irini, *International Law and the Protection of People at Sea* (Oxford: OUP, 2018).

Papanicolopulu, Irini, "The Duty to Rescue at Sea, in Peacetime and in War: A General Overview," *International Review of the Red Cross* 98 (2016): 491–514.

Papanicolopulu, Irini, "Immigrazione irregolare via mare, tutela della vita umana e organizzazioni non governative," *Diritto, Immigrazione e cittadinanza* 3 (2017): 1–29.

Papastavridis, Efthymios, "The Aquarius Incident and the Law of the Sea: Is Italy in Violation of the Relevant Rules?," *EJIL: Talk!*, June 27, 2018.

Papastavridis, Efthymios, "EUNAVFOR MED Operation Sophia and the Question of Jurisdiction over Transnational Organized Crime at Sea," *Questions of International Law, Zoom-in* 30 (2016): 19–34.

Papastavridis, Efthymios, "EUNAVFOR MED Operation Sophia: Fighting Smuggling of Migrants or Protecting Human Rights?," in *Protecting Human Rights in the European Union's External Relations*, ed. Sara Poli (The Hague: Cleer, 2016), 139–153.

Papastavridis, Efthymios, "EUNAVFOR Operation Sophia and the International Law of the Sea," *Maritime Safety and Security Law Journal* 2 (2016): 57–72.

Papastavridis, Efthymios, "EUNAVFOR Operation *Atalanta* off Somalia: The EU in Unchartered Legal Waters?," *International and Comparative Law Quarterly* 64 (2015): 533–568.

Papastavridis, Efthymios, "The Use of Force at Sea in the 21st Century: Some Reflections on the Proper Legal Framework(s)," *Journal of Territorial and Maritime Studies* 2 (2015): 119–138.

Papastavridis, Efthymios, "Is There a Right to Be Rescued at Sea? A Skeptical View," *Questions of International Law, Zoom-in* 4 (2014): 17–32.

Papastavridis, Efthymios, "European Convention of Human Rights and the Law of the Sea: The Strasbourg Court in Unchartered Waters?," in *The Interpretation and Application of the European Convention of Human Rights: Legal and Practical Implications*, eds. Malgosia Fitzmaurice and Panos Merkouris (Leiden: Nijhoff, 2013), 117–145.

Papastavridis, Efthymios, *The Interception of Vessels on the High Seas. Contemporary Challenges to the Legal Order of the Oceans* (Oxford: Hart, 2013).

Papastavridis, Efthymios, "Rescuing 'Boat People' in the Mediterranean Sea: The Responsibility of States under the Law of the Sea," *EJIL: Talk!*, May 31, 2011.

Papastavridis, Efthymios, "Enforcement Jurisdiction in the Mediterranean Sea: Illicit Activities and the Rule of Law on the High Seas," *International Journal of Marine and Coastal Law* 25 (2010): 569–599.

Papastavridis, Efthymios, "European Court of Human Rights Medvedyev and Others v. France (Grand Chamber, Application No. 3394/03) Judgment of 29 March 2010," *International and Comparative Law Quarterly* 59 (2010): 867–882.

Papastavridis, Efthymios, "'Fortress Europe' and Frontex: Within or without International Law?," *Nordic Journal of International Law* 79 (2010): 75–111.

Pascale, Giuseppe, "Is Italy Internationally Responsible for the Gross Human Rights Violations against Migrants in Libya?," *Questions of International Law, Zoom-in* 56 (2019): 35–58.

Passalacqua, Virginia, "The 'Open Arms' case: Reconciling the Notion of 'Place of Safety' with the Human Rights of Migrants," *EJIL: Talk!*, May 21, 2018.

Petrig, Anna, "Arrest, Detention and Transfer of Piracy Suspects: A Critical Appraisal of the German Courier Case Decision," in *Insecurity at Sea: Piracy and Other Risks to Navigation*, eds. Gemma Andreone, Giorgia Bevilacqua, Giuseppe Cataldi and Claudia Cinelli (Naples: Giannini, 2013), 153–171.

Piedimonte Bodini, Stefano, "Fighting Maritime Piracy under the European Convention on Human Rights," *European Journal of International Law* 22 (2011): 829–848.

Pisillo Mazzeschi, Riccardo, 'Due diligence' *e responsabilità internazionale degli Stati* (Milan: Giuffrè, 1989).

Quigley, John, "Complicity in International Law: A New Direction in the Law of State Responsibility," *British Yearbook of International Law* 57 (1987): 77–131.

Ratcovich, Martin, "The Concept of 'Place of Safety': Yet Another Self-Contained Maritime Rule or a Sustainable Solution to the Ever-Controversial Question of Where to Disembark Migrants Rescued at Sea," *Australian Yearbook of International Law* 33 (2015): 81–129.

Raymond, Catherine Zara, "Piracy and Armed Robbery in the Malacca Strait. A Problem Solved?," *Naval War College Review* 62 (2009): 30–42.

Rijpma, Jorrit, "Hybrid Agencification in the Area of Freedom, Security and Justice and Its Inherent Tensions: The Case of Frontex," in *The Agency Phenomenon in the European Union: Emergence, Institutionalization and Everyday Decision-Making*, eds. Madalina Busuioc, Martijn Groenleer and Jarle Trondal (Manchester: Manchester University Press, 2012), 84–101.

Ronzitti, Natalino, "Libia, raid americani e titubanze italiane," *Affari Internazionali*, August 9, 2016.

Ronzitti, Natalino, "The *Enrica Lexie* Incident: Law of the Sea and Immunity of State Official Issues," *Italian Yearbook of International Law* 22 (2012): 3–22.

Rosenberg, Lory Diana, "The Courts and Interception: The US Interdiction Experience and Its Impact on Refugees and Asylum Seekers," *Georgetown Immigration Law Journal* 17 (2003): 199–219.

Rosenne, Shabtai and Sohn, Louis (eds.), *United Nations Convention on the Law of the Sea. A Commentary* (Leiden: Nijhoff, 1982).

Rossi, Lucia Serena, "La sentenza del Bundesverfassungericht sul Trattato di Lisbona e le implicazioni sul processo di integrazione europea," in *Studi degli allievi di Paolo Mengozzi*, eds. Lucia Serena Rossi and Elisa Baroncini (Naples: Scientifica, 2010), 91–116.

Ryngaert, Cedric, *Jurisdiction in International Law* (2nd edn. Oxford: OUP, 2015).

Ryngaert, Cedric, "Apportioning Responsibility between the UN and Member States in UN Peace-Support Operations: An Inquiry into the Application of the 'Effective Control' Standard after *Behrami*," *Israel Law Review* 45 (2012): 151–178.

Ryngaert, Cedric, "The Immunity of International Organizations before Domestic Courts: Recent Trends," *International Organizations Law Review* 7 (2010): 121–148.

Salerno, Francesco, "International Responsibility for the Conduct of 'Blue Helmets': Exploring the Organic Link," in *Responsibility of International Organizations. Essays in Memory of Sir Ian Brownlie*, ed. Maurizio Ragazzi (Leiden: Nijhoff, 2013), 415–427.

Salerno, Francesco, "Treaties Establishing Objective Regimes," in *The Law of Treaties beyond the Vienna Convention*, ed. Enzo Cannizzaro (Oxford: OUP, 2011), 225–243.

Salerno, Francesco, "L'obbligo internazionale di *non-refoulement* dei richiedenti asilo," *Diritti umani e diritto internazionale* 4 (2010): 487–515.

Salvadego, Laura, "Controllo marittimo dell'immigrazione clandestina e giurisdizione penale del giudice italiano," *Rivista di diritto internazionale* 93 (2010): 1154–1159.

Sari, Aurel and Wessel, Ramses, "International Responsibility for EU Military Operations: Finding the EU's Place in the Global Accountability Regime," in *The EU's Role in Global Governance*, eds. Bart Van Vooren, Steven Blockmans and Jan Wouters (Oxford: OUP, 2013), 126–141.

Sari, Aurel, "The Conclusion of International Agreements by the European Union in the Context of ESDP," *International and Comparative Law Quarterly* 57 (2007): 53–86.

Schabas, William, *The European Convention on Human Rights: A Commentary* (Oxford: OUP, 2015).

Schusterschitz, Gregor, "European Agencies as Subjects of International Law," *International Organizations Law Review* 1 (2004): 163–188.

Scovazzi, Tullio, "La tutela della vita umana in mare, con particolare riferimento agli immigrati clandestini diretti verso l'Italia," *Rivista di diritto internazionale* 88 (2005): 106–120.

Simma, Bruno, Khan, Daniel-Erasmus, Nolte, Georg and Paulus, Andreas (eds.), *The Charter of the United Nations: A Commentary* (3rd edn. Oxford: OUP, 2012).

Simmonds, Robert, *Legal Problems Arising from the United Nations Operation in the Congo* (The Hague: Nijhoff, 1968).

Sommario, Emanuele, "Attribution of Conduct in the Framework of CSDP Missions: Reflections on a Recent Judgment by the Higher Administrative Court of

Nordrhein-Westfalen," in *Protecting Human Rights in the European Union's External Relations*, ed. Sara Poli (The Hague: Cleer, 2016), 155–174.

Spagnolo, Andrea, "Di intese segrete e alibi parlamentari: tra la decisione del TAR sull'accordo col Niger e il Global Compact sulle migrazioni," *SIDI Blog*, December 5, 2018.

Spagnolo, Andrea, *L'attribuzione delle condotte illecite nelle operazioni militari dell'Unione Europea* (Naples: Scientifica, 2016).

Spiezia, Filippo, "Traffico di migranti via mare: le linee guida della Direzione nazionale antimafia per la soluzione dei problemi di giurisdizione penale e di intervento cautelare nei casi di attraversamento di acque internazionali," *Diritto penale contemporaneo* (2014).

Steinhilper, Elias and Gruijters, Rob, "Border Deaths in the Mediterranean: What We Can Learn from the Latest Data," *Border Criminologies Blog*, March 8, 2017.

Tanaka, Yoshifumi, *The International Law of the Sea* (Cambridge: CUP, 2012).

Tancredi, Antonello, "Di pirati e Stati 'falliti': il Consiglio di sicurezza autorizza il ricorso alla forza nelle acque territoriali della Somalia," *Rivista di diritto internazionale* 91 (2008): 937–966.

Thouvenin, Jean-Marc, "Responsibility in the Context of the European Union Legal Order," in *The Law of International Responsibility*, eds. James Crawford, Alain Pellet and Simon Olleson (Oxford: OUP, 2010).

Thym, Daniel, "Transfer Agreements for Pirates Concluded by the EU. A Case Study on the Human Rights Accountability of the Common Security and Defence Policy," in *The Law and Practice of Piracy at Sea: European and International Perspectives*, eds. Panos Koutrakos and Achilles Skordas (Oxford: Hart, 2014), 167–181.

Tondini, Matteo, "The Use of Force in the Course of Maritime Law Enforcement Operations," *Journal on the Use of Force and International Law* 4 (2017): 253–272.

Tondini, Matteo, "Stato di diritto e lotta alla pirateria nelle acque somale," *Diritto penale e processo* 19 (2013): 230–245.

Treves, Tullio, "Human Rights and the Law of the Sea," *Berkeley Journal of International Law* 28 (2010): 1–14.

Treves, Tullio, "Piracy, Law of the Sea, and Use of Force: Developments off the Coast of Somalia," *European Journal of International Law* 20 (2009): 399–414.

Treves, Tullio, "The Rome Convention for the Suppression of Unlawful Acts against the Safety of Maritime Navigation," in *Maritime Terrorism and International Law*, ed. Natalino Ronzitti (Dordrecht: Nijhoff, 1990), 69–89.

Trevisanut, Seline, "Recognizing the Right to be Rescued at Sea," *Ocean Yearbook* 31 (2017): 137–154.

Trevisanut, Seline, "Is There a Right to Be Rescued at Sea? A Constructive View," *Questions of International Law, Zoom-in* 4 (2014): 3–15.

Trevisanut, Seline, "Search and Rescue Operations in the Mediterranean: Factor of Cooperation or Conflict?," *International Journal of Marine and Coastal Law* 25 (2010): 523–542.

Trevisanut, Seline, "Immigrazione clandestina via mare e cooperazione fra Italia e Libia dal punto di vista del diritto del mare," *Diritti umani e diritto internazionale* 3 (2009): 609–620.

Trevisanut, Seline, "The Principle of *Non-Refoulement* at Sea and the Effectiveness of Asylum Protection," *Max Planck Yearbook of United Nations Law* 12 (2008): 205–246.

Tzevelekos, Vassilis and Proukaki, Elena Katselli, "Migrants at Sea: A Duty of Plural States to Protect (Extraterritorially)?," *Nordic Journal of International Law* 86 (2017): 427–469.

Ventrella, Matilde, "The Impact of Operation Sophia on the Exercise of Criminal Jurisdiction against Migrant Smugglers and Human Traffickers," *Questions of International Law, Zoom-in* 30 (2016): 3–18.

Villani, Ugo, "Gli sviluppi del Trattato di Lisbona in materia di politica estera e di sicurezza comune," *Studi sull'integrazione europea* 6 (2011): 9–23.

Vitiello, Daniela, "La cooperazione operativa tra Frontex e i Paesi terzi nel contrasto all'immigrazione irregolare," in *Le migrazioni in Europa: UE, Stati terzi e migration outsourcing*, ed. Francesco Cherubini (Rome: Bordeaux, 2015), 163–271.

Wessel, Ramses and den Hertogh, Leonhard, "EU Foreign Security and Defence Policy: A Competence-Responsibility Gap?," in *The International Responsibility of the European Union: European and International Perspectives*, eds. Malcolm Evans and Panos Koutrakos (Oxford: Hart, 2013), 339–357.

Wiesenbach, Frederic, "Uncertainty on Somalia's Beaches. The Legal Regime of Onshore Anti-Piracy Operations," *Journal of Conflict and Security Law* 19 (2014): 85–112.

Wolfrum, Rüdiger, "Obligation of Result Versus Obligation of Conduct: Some Thoughts about the Implementation of International Obligations," in *Looking to the Future: Essays on International Law in Honor of Michael Reisman*, eds. Mahnoush Arsanjani and William Michael Reisman (Leiden: Nijhoff, 2011), 363–383.

Wolfrum, Rüdiger, "The Decentralized Prosecution of International Offences Through National Courts," in *War Crimes in International Law*, eds. Yoram Dinstein and Mala Tabory (The Hague: Nijhoff, 1996).

Wouters, Cornelis Wolfram and Den Heijer, Maarten, "The Marine I Case: A Comment," *International Journal of Refugee Law* 22 (2010): 1–19.

Zamuner, Enrico, *La tutela delle navi private nel diritto internazionale* (Naples: Scientifica, 2015).

Zwanenburg, Marten Coenraad, *Accountability of Peace-Support Operations* (Leiden: Nijhoff, 2005).

www.ingramcontent.com/pod-product-compliance
Lightning Source LLC
Chambersburg PA
CBHW031328230926
51848CB00001B/143
9789004408340